Contemplative Thoughts of an Asian Seminarian

Seamus Phan+

Contemplative Thoughts of an Asian Seminarian

Copyright©2007-2009 Fr. Seamus Phan+

Published by

Saint Flannan's Communion

All rights reserved. No part of this book may be reproduced in whole or in part without written permission from the publisher, except by reviewers who may quote brief excerpts in connection with a review in a newspaper, magazine, or electronic publication; nor may any part of this book be reproduced, stored in a retrieval system, or transmitted in any form or by any means electronic, mechanical, photocopying, recording, or other, without written permission from the publisher.

ISBN-13: 978-0-6152-1169-5

ISBN-10: 0-615-21169-0

1. Bible. Interpretation, commentary. 2. Theology. 3. Liturgy and rites. I. Phan, Seamus. II. Title.

9 8 7 6 5 4 3 2 1

Printed in the United States of America

Table of Contents

Table of Contents 1
Acknowledgments 3
Introduction 5
Christian Denominations 8
Contemplation and the Pastor 22
Early Christian Thought 38
CS Lewis and Mere Christianity 58
Christian Theology Primer 78
Charismas and Contemporary Changes 106
On Sacraments and their purposes 118
Constantine and Christianity 128
Reflections: Matrimony and Monasticism 140
    In the Old and New Testaments 140
    Theologies of the Fathers 144
    Laical and Monastic Christian Life 148
On Discipleship 158
Showing the face of God in the East 168
    Christian influence in China 169
    The difficulties of evangelizing in Asia 169
    The Nestorian influence during the Tang dynasty 173
    Matteo Ricci's success during the Ming dynasty 174
    Learning from Matteo Ricci 176
    Becoming the Confucian gentleman 176
    Using secular knowledge to influence the authorities .. 178
    Educating the gentiles on the path of God 179
    Syncretism and guarding against it 180
    What syncretism is, or is not 181
    Guarding against syncretism in Asia 182

    Finding common ground with an ecumenical heart 182
    Common ground and orthodoxy 184
    Using tiered strategy of W.E.B. 190
    Works - Humanitarian works, funding and helping 190
    Evangelism - To the spiritually seeking 192
    Brotherhood - Bonding with the accomplished 193
    Problem-solving during evangelism 195
    Evangelizing process - groups or individual 195
    Historical - fact-finding and investigating 196
    Obstacle - Explore questions, doubts, and concerns 198
    Projection – Witnessing and anticipating results 204
    End-results of successful conversion, or open dialog 206
    Styles of influencing 207
    Persuasive style of influence 209
    Cooperative or compromising style of influence 210
    Aggressive style of influence 211
    Suggested mechanics of persuasion 212
    Conclusions 217
Bibliography 223
Index 231
About the Author 233

Acknowledgments

The author has gained tremendous inspiration and learning from (not in any order of importance):

First of all, exalted God, for He has shown his kindest grace to me during my most doubting and troubled times, and gave me peace and wisdom to take on this path in His glory. He also made the path to completing my seminary studies such a blessed journey.

And to all of these mentors and friends who made my path blessed and comforting (in alphabetical order), ++Abp. Frederick Burcklé, Dr. Douglass Capogrossi, Pr. Laurent Cleenewerck, Rev. Ken Collins, ++Abp. Anthony Cowles, +Bp. John R. Dillard, Dr. Al Erisman, Rev. Oscar Flores, Dr. Kenneth James, Dr. Glenn Mollette, John Rapp, +Fr. Dmitri Ross, +Dom Klaus Schlapps, Rev. Sng Chong Hui, Dr. Sylvan Keith Wilhite, ++Abp. Michael Wrenn, Christian Chaplains Association, Spiritual Directors International, and my supportive family.

Introduction

I have been raised as a Buddhist, even though both my parents were schooled in Christian thought when they were much younger.

Throughout my youth, my curious mind wanted very much to know just what life meant, and what we should seek to become. I was open to new ideas, and studied various scriptures and texts of the mainstream faiths, including Buddhism (Theraveda, Mahayana and Vajrayana), Taoism, Confucianism, Christianity, Hinduism, etc. It was difficult to find answers I could reconcile with at the mission school I attended, because the presiding pastor did not manage to answer many of the questions I raised. However, I found Buddhism very intellectually challenging and it appealed to the philosopher in me.

Sometime in late 2004, I faced tremendous challenges when I was involved in a rather uphill struggle against someone who sought to destroy my life. It was a hellish period when I realized who the pretenders in my life were, and also, who some of my truest friends were.

Just when I contemplated various depressing thoughts, God showed His grace to me, through rather gentle miracles that led me to pursue Him and find out more. He presented various people in the form of senior Christian clergy, who were involved in various humanitarian causes I was volunteering with. Their kind, gentle and non-abrasive ways impressed upon me that Christianity can also be a calming force, not quite the fervent "you are damned if you don't believe" kind of preaching I heard in my youth.

Through these experienced and enlightened Christian clergy, I yearned to find out more about God, and eventually, went on to study my doctor of theology at a small seminary. I could only attribute the seemingly effortless journey at the seminary to the grace of God, as He made many things possible, and made the learning journey enjoyable, stimulating, and heart-warming.

God called out to me to serve, which I rejected, on many occasions. I felt I was not ready, and was not worthy of such a serious path. However, if no mortal can be perfect, then I should not reject God's call and should allow Him to make all things work in His glory. I was eventually ordained as a minister under the Lutheran tradition, and has gone on to study more in the areas of liturgy and pre-Nicene theology. I have also been warmly welcomed by and in communion with Wesleyan and Celtic traditions.

Today, I am an itinerant minister, and also focus on the preparation and writing of Christian works, and prayers for people in adversity. It is my humble belief that faith during the worst of adversity, is the most curative and transforming.

I am but a student of theology, and the road is long. There are many human errors, all of which are mine to bear, in this humble work. And since our Christian path is such a rich, varied tradition, there may invariably be theological differences, of which I humbly ask for your brotherhood in Christ always. I sincerely hope that these humble writings of my time at the seminary, can be useful in some small way to you. In the name of our Lord Jesus Christ, I wish you peace always.

Your brother in Christ,

Fr. Seamus+

Christian Denominations

Christian Denominations

Abstract

Dr. Ron Rhodes, President of Reasoning from the Scriptures Ministries, a non-profit, has authored thirty-five books on apologetics and Christian ministry. In this book, Dr Rhodes attempt to distill the mainstream Christian denominations, from the Roman Catholic Church, the Eastern Orthodox Church, and the Protestant churches, into an easy to understand and reference volume. Rhodes' past books focus on apologetic ministry and preaching, and his views are often staunch and stern, with little tolerance for views outside the orthodox. While denominational differences can sometimes be important in following the road to God, it is also important to dissect Rhodes' book to provide a more ecumenical baseline so that tolerance among Christian brethren can work for the betterment for the universal church of God.

Dr Rhodes began the book with a brief summary of how various Christian denominations came about, and following chapters discussed denominations such as: Adventist, Baptist, Brethren, Catholic, Christian, Congregational, Episcopal and Anglican (or Church of England), Friends (Quaker), Fundamentalist and Bible, Holiness, Lutheran, Mennonite, Methodist, Orthodox, Pentecostal, Presbyterian, and Reformed churches, in alphabetical order. We will briefly outline some of the movements in this paper.

Rhodes started with the definition and the emergence of the term "Christians", first quoted in Antioch, for those who were disciples of Jesus Christ, around 42 AD. The term Christians thus differentiated others who believed in Judaism (even as the same Old Testament is shared) or other monotheistic religions of the world, as being those who had a personal relationship with Jesus Christ. Even as disciples of Christ did not use the word "Christianity" to describe their movement, the word "Christianity" began to emerge around the time of the Roman Augustine, a good many centuries after, around 354 AD onwards. Rhodes did not believe the concept of a "church" existed in the Old Testament, and believed that Matthew 16:18 quoted Jesus as saying "I will build my church", with the key word "will" being to mean in the future. However, that opinion may not be universally accepted.

Rhodes made a simplified but clear distinction of several religious leaders who influenced the evolution of Christianity, including Pope Leo I (400-461 AD) who first made claims of papal authority; Michael Caerularius (1058 AD), Patriarch of Constantinople whose Eastern Orthodox church broke from the Roman Catholic church; and Augustinian monk Dr Martin Luther (1483-1546 AD), the German reformer and founder of the Lutheran movement, who can be seen as the start of Protestantism, as well as King Henry VIII (1509-1547 AD), who broke away from the Roman Catholic church with the start of the Anglican and Episcopal movement under the Church of England.

Rhodes made a short distinction of the Protestants, which started in the sixteenth century, which hoped to bring reform to the church. According to history, the Diet of Speyer first coined the word "Protestant" in 1529, having granted tolerance to the Lutherans, the movement started by Dr Martin Luther. Eventually, the term "Protestant" became a common term to describe any Christian movement that separated from the Roman Catholic or Eastern Orthodox Church, or those that were independently developed. As of 2000 AD, about one-fifth of all Christians are Protestant, with the Roman Catholic Church still the largest Christian movement in the world today.

In Rhodes book, he quoted Robert McAfee, in his book "The Spirit of Protestantism", which took a more positive approach to the meaning of the word "Protestant":

> *The verb "to protest" comes from the Latin pro-testari, and means not only "to testify", but, more important, "to testify on behalf of something." Webster's Dictionary gives as a synonym, "to affirm". The Oxford English Dictionary defines it, "to declare formally in public, testify, to make a solemn declaration."*

Other Protestant leaders mentioned by Rhodes include John Calvin (1509-1564 AD), the French reformer whose Calvinist movement led to the coming of Presbyterian and Reformed churches, John Wesley (1703-1791 AD), an Anglican minister who started the Methodist movement. Three individuals were credited by Rhodes to have been instrumental in the beginning of the Fundamentalist movement, include Dwight L Moody (1837-1899 AD), John Nelson Darby (1800-1882 AD), and Cyrus Scofield (1843-1921 AD). Another personality mentioned in the book was William J Seymour (1870-1922 AD), whose evangelistic movement in Los Angeles, USA, led to the rise of the Pentecostal movement.

The Adventist movement's theology was detailed to talk about a different chronology of our world, with 457 BC as the beginning of the world, according to Adventist founder William Miller (Rhodes 2005, 22). Miller also believed that the world would come to an end on March 21, 1844, which of course did not happen. That view led to the schism within the Adventist movement, although Miller did apologize for his error but still held on to the belief that the world will be destroyed imminently, as well as the second coming of Jesus Christ. Miller talked about two resurrections, that of believers at the second coming of Christ, that of unbelievers after the millennium, and departed believers will not enter heaven in soul and spirit until the final blessedness of the second coming of Christ.

The Baptist movement did not have a clear-cut lineage, although Rhodes mentioned three possibilities, that the Baptist movement started (1) as early as John the Baptist; (2) from Anabaptist[1] origins from Germany, Holland and Switzerland; and (3) from English separatists in the seventeenth-century, who believed that the church should be made up of only regenerate membership (born-again), whereby adult baptism is the only valid form of baptism. Baptists are largely Arminian[2] in theology, that Jesus Christ died for all people and that salvation is possible for everyone (unlike Calvinist[3] theology which described the elected or selected people without foreknowledge). The second possible lineage from Anabaptist movements is largely disputed, as Anabaptists and Baptists have key theological differences. For example, Anabaptists are averse to oaths and public office, unlike Baptists. Anabaptists also believe in the apostolic succession in the administration of baptism (similar to Roman Catholic, Old Catholic and Eastern Orthodox movements), which the larger Protestant movement does not subscribe to.

---

[1] Anabaptists believe that infants who were baptized must be re-baptized when they reach adulthood, having a mature profession of faith.
[2] Arminian theology stressed on election based on foreknowledge, unlimited atonement for all people, the inability of humans to save themselves and need the Holy Spirit to cleanse and create a "new birth", prevenient Grace of the Holy Spirit to allow humans to yearn to learn the gospel and lean to God for salvation, and conditional perseverance of believers (whereby people have to continuously seek the Grace of God and walk in the light, rather than turn from Grace).
[3] Calvinist theology stressed on the total depravity of humans, unconditional election of certain persons to salvation, limited atonement of Christ (only for the elect), irresistible Grace (versus the human will), and the perseverance of the Saints.

The largest Christian denomination, including in this part of Asia, would have to be the Roman Catholic Church (ibid, 95). The Roman Catholic Church is generally perceived as "the" Catholic church, although other Catholic movements exist. The Roman Catholic Church is headed by the Pope (otherwise known as "vicar of Christ") in Vatican City, a sovereign entity within Italy. The first Pope to claim authority over all other churches was Pope Leo I in the fourth century. One of the key theological differences between the Roman Catholic Church and Protestant churches lie in the Bible version itself. Protestant bibles tend to contain the Old Testament and the New Testament only, while Catholic bibles contain additional texts known as the Apocrypha, seven complete books and four partial books, which originated between the Old and New Testament periods. The Roman Catholic church also differs from the Protestant churches in the sacraments, whereby Catholics believe there are seven sacraments, that of Baptism, penance, the Eucharist (or Latin Rite Mass), confirmation, matrimony, holy orders, and the anointing of the sick. Catholic sacraments are seen as containers of God's grace, which infuses the believer when involved in the sacraments. The Roman Catholic movement has within itself, several theological differences. The most traditional of Roman Catholics reject the Vatican II[4] reforms, while traditional

---

[4] Vatican II reform, otherwise known as the Second Ecumenical Council of the Vatican, was started by Pope John XXIII in 1962 and completed by Pope Paul VI in 1965, hoped to bring reform to the Roman Catholic Church and ecumenical reconciliation with the Eastern Orthodox Church and Judaism. However, because the Vatican II's Lumen Gentium document talked about ecumenism and liturgy reform with believers outside the Roman Catholic tradition, some traditionalists were in disagreement with Lumen Gentium, citing that it ran counter to the belief that the Roman Catholic church is the one and only true Christian church founded by Jesus Christ, as well as eroding the Latin Rite Mass of the Roman Catholic church. (Wikipedia, Internet, 2007)

Roman Catholics are critical of the more liberal stances within the church but accept the Vatican II reform. The Roman Catholic Church is the more commonly known Catholic order, while the Eastern Rite Catholic church and Old Catholic church are some others. The Eastern Rite Catholic church (ibid, 105) is basically the Eastern Orthodox Church orders, which went back to communion with the Roman Catholic Church, while maintaining the original Eastern Rites, and married clergy. Roman Catholic clergy cannot be married. The Old Catholic church, which was founded in 1871, came about when Swiss, German and Austrian priests were excommunicated from the Roman Catholic Church when they denounced the concept of papal infallibility established during the First Vatican Council (1870). Old Catholic churches conform to the Declaration of Utrecht (ibid, 107). Some Old Catholic churches are monastic in nature.

The Anglican (ibid, 137) or Episcopal[5] Church started from the Church of England by King Henry VIII (1509-1547 AD). King Henry VIII was already married to Catherine of Aragon, but she bore him only a daughter and he badly needed a male heir. King Henry VIII then asked Pope Clement VII to allow him to divorce Catherine, but the pope denied the king's request. So King Henry VIII convinced his parliament to erect laws that denied the pope any authority or jurisdiction over the Church of England, while granting himself, a king, sovereign authority over his church, turning the Church of England into a "state church". Then King Henry promptly appointed Thomas Cranmer (1489-1556 AD) as the Archbishop of Canterbury and Archbishop granted King Henry his annulment of marriage to Catherine. The Episcopal Church in America is today an independent denomination from the Church of

---

[5] Episcopal means, "governed by bishops".

England (since the church is not governed by the state in America), but all of which are in full communion under the Worldwide Anglican Communion.

The Fundamentalist (ibid, 171) movement started to counter the assertions of the liberal Christian movements, by holding on to the fundamental principles and doctrines of Christianity, such as the Bible as infallible, the deity of Jesus Christ as God incarnate under the Triune God, and died for our sins, humanity as born of sin, creationism, and so on. One of the more well known fundamentalists was John Nelson Darby (1800-1882 AD), whose dispensationalist approach meant that he believed the Jews to be the elect and even as they do not accept Christ as savior, God has a special favor for the Jews, which will be revealed during the Dispensation (or Church Age).

The Lutheran (ibid, 211) movement, led by Dr Martin Luther (1483-1546 AD), can be considered the starting point of the Protestant movement. Luther switched from legal studies, to theological studies, and completed his doctoral work at the age of 28. While teaching at the University of Wittenberg in 1517, Luther was said to have nailed his proclamation document, the "95 Theses" (CRTA, Internet, 2007), in protest against the Roman Catholic Church and specific practices such as his protest of indulgences (Wikipedia, 2007), which although Luther was very religious, could not agree with. Luther's contributions included the Lutheran Large Catechism and Small Catechism, and his followers later compiled his thinking into the Book of Concord (Book of Concord, Internet, 2007), which combined the Large and Small Catechisms of Luther, the Apostles' Creed[6], the Nicene Creed[7], the

---

[6] Apostles' Creed is one of the most used within the Reformed churches as a statement of faith, citing the belief in the Triune God, Christ's birth

Athanasian Creed[8], the Augsburg Confession (Book of Con, and the Smalcald Articles of Faith. One of the main differences between the Roman Catholic and the Lutheran view can be expressed through the Lord's Supper. The Roman Catholic view is that the bread and wine actually become transformed into the body and blood of Jesus during the prayer initiated by the presiding priest, with Jesus literally present during the event, and the sacrament gives grace to the believer. The Lutheran view takes a slightly different view in that Jesus is present in, with and under the bread and the wine, and His presence is real, but the substance of the bread and wine are not transformed. The event allows God to communicate grace to believers. The Reformed view, representing many Protestant traditions, believes simply that Jesus is spiritually present at the event and it is a means of God's grace. The more liberal traditions would go further to say that the bread and wine not only do not transform, do not communicate any grace to the believer either, but are merely symbolic reminders of Jesus' death and resurrection (ibid, 218).

The Methodist (ibid, 263) movement was started by John Wesley (1703-1791 AD) and younger brother Charles Wesley (1707-1788 AD), in England. The Wesleys came from a traditional Anglican household, and their father was an Anglican rector[9]. The brothers were both pious and steadfast in their religious practice, so much so that they

---

and death, and resurrection, and the belief in the Holy Spirit and the universal church. (CRTA, Internet, 2007).

[7] The Nicene Creed affirms the eternal pre-existence of Jesus Christ and in His divine nature as the Father (ibid, 220).

[8] The Athanasian Creed affirms the Triune God with equal majesty and glory (ibid, 220).

[9] Rector, in the Anglican sense, refers traditionally to parish priests who receive directly the tithes of his parish, while a vicar receives a fixed stipend. In the modern context, most people would simply refer to parish priests as vicars (Wikipedia, 2007).

were seen by peers and others as "methodical" in their religious practice, hence the latter name of the movement – Methodism. The brothers were different in their approach, whereby John Wesley was an evangelical preacher and Charles was famous in writing hymns, and was known for more than five and a half thousand hymns. The Church of England persecuted John Wesley and the Methodists as non-conformists, and John frequently preached in open fields. John Wesley also established the first instance of lay ministry, of allowing non-ordained laypeople to preach the gospel, and ultimately led to the popularity of the Methodist movement (and some would say open the grounds to lay ministry in the modern evangelistic movements). John Wesley also believed that apostolic succession was fiction, and later went on to ordain ministers independently. One of the main theological beliefs of the Methodists center on Arminian idea of human free will rather than Calvinists' concept of predestination and irresistible grace, and so has found appeal in many gentile nations, including Asia.

The Orthodox Church (ibid, 291) is one of the three main branches of Christianity, the others being Roman Catholic and Protestant. The main Orthodox churches include those from Russia, Ukraine, Bulgaria, Albania, Romania, Serbia, Greece and Cyprus. While the word "orthodox" does usually convey the notion of "true doctrine", the other meaning of "orthodox" means "true glory". The main differences that separates the Roman Catholic church and the Orthodox church is the Orthodox church's rejection of papal infallibility (especially "ex cathedra", when speaking from the chair of authority), indulgences, and the associated treasury of merits of saints in absolution of sin, purgatory (the process of purification after death even for believers, a notion Protestants also reject), the immaculate conception of Mary, and the assumption of Mary (whereby she was raised to Heaven in body and soul in union). The Orthodox church also differs from the Protestant churches in that rather than seeing the Bible as all important, the Orthodox church sees itself as the custodian and key interpreter of the Bible.

The Pentecostal (ibid, 311) movement is often secularly associated with the "speaking of tongues". More accurately, the Pentecostal movement believes that the Holy Spirit's baptism is accompanied by the gift of glossolalia (that of speaking a language that is alien or unknown to the person speaking) (Wikipedia, 2007), considered as a second work of grace, or the "second blessing". Pentecostal Christians draws the speaking of tongues from the New Testament book of Acts, as a miracle of the Pentecost, whereby Jesus' apostles spoke in languages alien to them so as to preach to an audience of diverse linguistic backgrounds.

The Presbyterian (ibid, 341) and Reformed (ibid, 365) movements were both influenced and inspired by John Calvin (1509-1564 AD), although the Presbyterian movement was actually founded by John Knox (1513-1572 AD), a Scottish theologian. The name Presbyterian comes from the Greek word "presbuteros", which means "elder", since such churches are led by elders (or presbyters). Since both the Presbyterian and Reformed churched are heavily influenced by Calvin, their churches believe in the concept of "election by sovereignty", where God's sovereign act, chooses certain individuals to salvation before the formation. This runs contrary to the Arminian view that God's election is based on His foreknowledge of who would respond favorably to the gospel. The Reformed movement generally subscribes to the Belgic Confession[10], the

---

[10] Guido de Bres wrote the Belgic Confession in 1561 to confront King Philip of Span that reformed theology was biblical and not heretical.

Heidelberg Catechism[11], and the Canons of Dordt[12], as statements of faith.

Top 5 Themes and Why

Rhodes opening chapter (ibid, 7) served to describe the evolution of the universal church and the schism of theology within the three main streams of Roman Catholicism, Orthodox Church, and the Protestant Church in general. The opening chapter was very important to establish some of the key differences between the different mainstream thoughts, with the theme of how the contemporary church we know of, came about.

The second theme that the author believes to be important was the segregation of Calvinist and Arminian theology, in the separation of the concept of election. This separates many mainstream Protestant churches.

The third theme that was important is the description of the breakaway of Martin Luther and King Henry VIII, together with other Reformists, from the Roman Catholic Church. This series of historical events prompted the rise of the Protestant movement, with many brilliant theologians along the way to define (and sometimes separate) the reformed thinking.

The fourth theme that the author felt was important was the breaking away of the Orthodox Church from the Roman Catholic Church. The differences between the theological thinking between these traditions still separate these two very traditional mainstream paths to God.

---

[11] The Heidelberg Catechism was written by Zacharias Ursinus and Caspar Olevianus in 1563 in the ecumenical hope of bringing Lutheran and Reformed theology together.

[12] The Synod of Dordt in the city of Dordrecht wrote the Canons of Dordt in 1618 to 1619, to discuss predestination and God's sovereignty and works of salvation, all related to Calvinistic theology (CRTA, Internet, 2007).

The fifth theme which the author felt is important is the rise of the Pentecostal movement, which continues to influence many mainstream churches, and the charismatics of the Pentecostal movement seem to influence especially the younger generation, which the author observe in his regional travels and research.

Author's Notes

Rhodes book serves as an important primer into the complex world of theological differences, which the author believes to be important differentiators to different believers (or pre-believers).

For example, for ministering to traditionalists and those who would prefer classical approaches, a contemporary or charismatic approach or theology, may not be easily accepted by them. Conversely, a younger person who is attuned to modern influences of the Internet, multimedia and modern music influences, may not be easily persuaded by the liturgy of the traditional churches. The author is ecumenical and recognizes that perhaps everyone needs a different pathway to God, and that Rhodes book opens up a comprehensive and succinct window to allow anyone to quickly explain theological differences, and different churches, to believers, new believers, or non-believers alike.

Contemplation and the Pastor

Contemplation and the Pastor

Abstract

Reverend Eugene Peterson is an accomplished theologian, and has served as Professor Emeritus of Spiritual Theology, Regent College at Seattle Pacific University, New York Theological Seminary, and John Hopkins University. He is a founding pastor for Christ Our King Presbyterian Church in Bel Air, Maryland, and has preached there for twenty-nine years.

Professor Peterson has written more than thirty books and audio-visual programs[13], including "Answering God – The Psalms as tools for prayer", "Eat This Book – A conversation in the art of spiritual reading", "Christ Plays in Ten Thousand Places – A conversation in spiritual theology", and many others, especially many that drew wisdom from Proverbs and Psalms.

The author has found the book "The Contemplative Pastor – Returning to the art of spiritual direction" by Peterson, a very thought provoking reminder of what pastoral counseling and ministry mean in a long process or life's journey. It is a gentle and yet firm reminder that being a pastor, especially over a long haul, separates us further from God. Peterson's book serves up inspired wisdom to return to our roots as believers, rather than simply doing God's work. He drew wisdom from the Beatitudes, and discussed themes of how to make "small talk" with the congregation, a return to a quiet prayer, and use personal examples. The book is written from the first-person perspective, and the author felt that the book came across with sincerity and quiet wisdom, and found it very useful in keeping vigil over one's ministry, especially when one faces challenges in working with difficult situations. Rather than being instructive or criticizing, Peterson shared wisdom like a brother, which made the book useful to pastors on a lifetime of ministry.

---

[13] Professor Eugene Peterson maintains a website, which shows the full range of books he authored and audiovisual programs, at www.eugenepetersononline.com.

Mr. Rodney Clapp, associate editor for Christianity Today, wrote the foreword (Peterson 1993, 1) to Reverend Peterson's book. One of the things which made Peterson different was his desire to remain with his parish of some 300 people for twenty-nine years, at a small church known as Christ Our King Presbyterian Church in Bel Air, Maryland. He retired in 1991. Peterson decided early that he would be a pastor to only as many people as he could remember them by name. This continuing ministry to a small congregation for so long, showed the steadfast demeanor of Peterson, and might lend a clue to not only this book, but many other contemplative books of Peterson.

Peterson split his book into three portions, "Redefinitions", "Between Sundays", and "The Word Made Fresh".

In the first portion "Redefinitions", Peterson discussed the need for a pastor to re-examine his or her own role as a pastor, especially in the need for a pastor to change from a benign but passive entity, to become one who is "unbusy" (Peterson 1993, 17), "subversive" (ibid, 27), and "apocalyptic" (ibid, 39).

In the second portion "Between Sundays", Peterson discussed the need for a pastor to move beyond simply ministering on Sundays, and spending the rest of the six days of a week simply to prepare for pulpit ministry. Rather, Peterson discussed the need for curing souls (ibid, 55), the need for praying without delusions or self-deception (ibid, 67), the need for artful language in the specific instances of ministry (ibid, 87), allowing God's will to work (ibid, 95), the need for making small talk in order to further one's ministry successfully (ibid, 111), the need to be non-judgmental as a pastor (ibid, 117), managing perceptions and expectations of a congregation (ibid, 129), and the need even for pastors to go for a sabbatical (ibid, 141).

The third portion of the book, Peterson wrote several poems dedicated to the reflective prayer, with a reference to how ancient prophets and psalmists were also poets. Peterson's poetry can be seen as simple and honest, without any façade of crafty language.

Before we discuss the book further, it is also important to discuss just what "spiritual direction" means.

According to Liz Budd Ellman, executive director Spiritual Directors International (SDI), an international non-profit organization based in Bellevue, Washington, said on the website[14],

> "*Spiritual direction is the process of accompanying people on a spiritual journey... Spiritual direction helps us learn how to live in peace, with compassion, promoting justice, as humble servants of that which lies beyond all names... Spiritual direction is not counseling. Spiritual direction is not therapy. Spiritual direction is not financial advice.*"

One evident quote from Peterson in his interaction with Clapp, in the Foreword of the book, showed just what spiritual direction meant to Peterson, and in what form and action he took in his ministry at Christ Our King Presbyterian Church,

> "*...My job is not to solve people's problems or make them happy, but to help them see the grace operating in their lives.*"

Spiritual direction in the context of a spiritual director can be more explicitly explained as follows[15]. It is a practice of being with people, sometimes individually, to help them

---

[14] What spiritual direction is, and is not (SDIworld.org, Internet, 2007).
[15] Spiritual direction explained in the form of a relationship between spiritual directors and people seeking direction (Wikipedia, 2007).

deepen their relationship with God. The person seeking direction will share personal encounters with God, and to relate some spiritual challenges. The spiritual director often will listen and ask questions that can help the person seeking direction, to reflect and contemplate on, and in so, find a closer bond with God. Often, spiritual direction is a personalized experience, and involves more interactive engagement than a community prayer or service.

Petersen described in the chapter "The Unbusy Pastor" (ibid, 17), of how contemporary pastors have frequently tried to pack daily or weekly schedules with ministry, preparatory work, counseling, and more. However, Peterson postulates that he has been busy for two "wrong" reasons – vanity, and laziness. Of vanity, Peterson painted the analogy of finding a doctor. He said that often, people would rather visit a doctor for an ailment if the doctor is extremely busy and there is a queue, rather than a doctor sitting in a quiet clinic. In his words, a busy pastor can be made to feel "important". Of laziness, Peterson explained that it seemed easier to simply relinquish the responsibility of a pastor to his congregation, by allowing the congregation to decide for the pastor what he or she should do.

To vanity and laziness that brings about busywork, Peterson proposed that a pastor could return to doing three important things – praying, preaching, and listening.

It came as no surprise that Peterson wrote that a pastor should first and foremost, pray, before preaching. A committed prayer allows the pastor to grow closer to God, and to allow God's grace to illuminate his pastoral duties. Peterson described the need for constant and committed prayer so that he would not live as a "parasite on the first-hand spiritual life of others" (ibid, 20). All too often, a pastor is called to pray for others, to lead in prayer, but Peterson made the assertion that a pastor should also pray, above any other pastoral duty. To Peterson, prayer should be done over the whole life, in a disciplined and deliberate time, away from the hustle and bustle of a noisy life.

Peterson then wrote that a pastor should preach (ibid, 20), and not just by delivering sermons that challenge the congregation to inspirational heights. To Peterson, simply developing a powerful sermon without strong orthodox biblical grounding is not in the best interests of a congregation. Therefore, in order to make preaching truly meaningful in the glory of God, Peterson asserted that again, peace and solitude is necessary, similar to prayer.

Next, a pastor should listen well (ibid, 21), rather than simply talking to his or her congregation. Again, Peterson asserted that in order to listen well to the congregation as a spiritual director, a pastor couldn't be hurried or busy.

Peterson then provided simple guidelines for a pastor to transform from "busy" to "unbusy", through the use of the appointment calendar. He wrote down and marked off all events such as prayer, reading, leisure, preaching, listening, so that his time can be respected by the congregation, segregating and giving due diligence time to each pastoral and personal activity. Peterson also closed the chapter with an interesting observation, that when a pastor leaves a congregation, the congregation often carries on rather well with a new pastor. This removes the vanity and ego of a pastor, to allow him or her to do the work of God as a servant of the Word without prejudice or vanity.

In the chapter "The Subversive Pastor" (ibid, 27) Peterson illustrated that in the contemporary world, the role of pastors has largely diminished to the sidelines, where corporate and material success is more frequently celebrated, rather than spirituality and piety. Peterson called on pastors to become "subversives", much as Jesus was a master of subversion. How did Jesus become a "subversive pastor"? He told parables and stories, which sounded mundane and simple, with powerful subliminal message within the stories. Peterson lamented that contemporary pastors have sometimes given up on subversive ministering and instead, turned to aggressive promotion of the gospel only. Yet, subversive ministering can be powerful, evidenced by passages in the Bible such as "You are the salt of the earth" (Matt. 5:13), which gave visual and poetic imagery to biblical meaning, rather than two-dimensional words forcibly catapulted at the congregation.

Peterson first explained that the word "apocalyptic" and "pastor" seem to be eternally divorced from each other in the chapter "The Apocalyptic Pastor" (ibid, 39), since "apocalyptic" implies an end-time context, while "pastor" tends to infer a much more positive experience. However, Peterson strongly urged pastors to take the mantle from Saint Paul, with a need to impress upon the congregation in no uncertain terms, that prayer and communion with God is the only salvation, without the need to mince words or be a "nice" pastor. Too often, people living in the secular and materialistic world drown in the many struggles and pursuits of secular life, and relegate God and spirituality to just a weekly routine on Sundays. Peterson's call to pastors to be apocalyptic is perhaps described as an uneasy necessity to bring believers to God.

Peterson then discussed the importance of spiritual direction and pastoral transformation or at least contemplation, between Sundays, in the section "Between Sundays" (ibid, 53). He emphasized that although Sundays are important in energizing people at church, the congregation can sometimes forget the many days between Sundays, as they go about their daily mundane livelihood. The inertia or inaction by pastors to address the six days after a Sunday can cause the congregation to lapse back into a decline or even lapses of spirituality. Sometimes, pastors become trapped with the "running of the church" between Sundays, rather than caring or curing for the souls of the congregation.

Peterson made a clear distinction between the running of a church, and the curing of souls. As a pastor serving in that functional role, he or she will be an executive to ensure that the church runs well, in so far as electricity is running, lights are working, premises are clean, the audiovisual facilities are working, Sunday reading materials are duplicated in sufficient numbers, and so on.

However, Peterson correctly stated that the curing of souls really depends on God's everlasting and always present grace. He wrote (ibid, 60),

"Prevenience is the conviction that God has been working diligently, redemptively, and strategically before I appeared on the scene, before I was aware there was something here for me to do."

Peterson then described the working language when running a church, and that of curing of souls. In running a church, he described the working language as one that is descriptive and motivational, descriptive so that the team can know precisely what tasks and resources are required to get things done, while motivational so that the lay team can be driven enough to complete the many myriad tasks, some of which may be deemed uninteresting.

In the curing of souls during spiritual direction, however, since intimate feelings and thoughts are revealed to the pastor, it is important that the working language be one of love and prayer. Therefore, prescriptive and instructive words would not work well during spiritual direction, while kinship, humane and comforting words, can mean a great deal to people.

In the chapter "Praying with eyes open" (ibid, 67), Peterson opened with a reference to John Calvin (1509-1564 AD) who gave us Calvinist[16] thought. Peterson thought Calvin to be peculiar in that although Calvin fully explained and taught the majesty of God's creation, calling it "a theater of God's glory", Calvin did not seem to spend much time outside Geneva, Switzerland where he stayed most of the time, nor talked much about the glorious scenery around him.

However, writer Annie Dillard[17] seemed to embrace God's glorious theater completely, according to Peterson. In her Pulitzer Prize[18] winning book "Pilgrim at Tinker Creek", she wrote,

> "*Divinity is not playful. The universe was not made in jest but in solemn incomprehensible earnest. By a power fathomably (sic) secret, and holy, and fleet. There is nothing to be done about it, but ignore it, or see.*"

In Peterson's interpretation of Annie Dillard's life view, it would appear he was emphasizing less of her awe and respect for all God's creation, but more importantly, to reverently pray and seek communion in God through the observance of all wondrous creation. Too often, people in hurried secular lives chasing after illusive and materialistic

---

[16] Calvinist theology stressed on the total depravity of humans, unconditional election of certain persons to salvation, limited atonement of Christ (only for the elect), irresistible Grace (versus the human will), and the perseverance of the Saints.

[17] Annie Dillard (born 1945) was a prolific writer who wrote about God through fiction, poetry and some non-fiction. She was professor emeritus at Wesleyan University. Two of her better-known works include "Tickets for a Prayer Wheel" (1974) and "Pilgrim at Tinker Creek" (1974). Anniedillard.com, Internet, 2007.

[18] Pulitzer Prize is an American award for literary or music composition achievements, administered by Columbia University in New York City. (Wikipedia, 2007).

pursuits can forget the majesty of God's universe, and neglect to realize there is Divine grace in all things.

In the chapter "First Language" (ibid, 89), Peterson described the need for pastors to return to what he called the "first language". He defined the "first language" as that of intimacy and relationship, while the "second language" is one of information, and the "third language" is one of motivation. Too often, pastors may oscillate between the use of the second or third language, juxtaposing information with bits of motivation, when addressing a congregation, or even during spiritual direction. However, Peterson mentioned that in order for spiritual direction to bring benefit for people, the language of prayer must be used, and the language of prayer is one of intimacy and relationship with God. In earnest honesty and emotive expression, the first language is perhaps seen as the only way to communicate with God, and with people, during spiritual direction.

In "Is Growth a Decision?" (ibid, 95), Peterson explored the concept of human will.

In the exploration of Peterson's own life, he told of his early secular life, having gone through many jobs, from the kitchen, workshop, to athletics, in a studio, were all what he said to be "apprenticeships in the work of God". In many mundane livelihoods, all too often, people get excited and sucked into an eternal and endless struggle for worldly recognition and material achievements. However, such pursuits can be said to be simply an enlargement of one's ego and an indulgence in one's self, rather than leaving them behind in a communion with God. In Peterson's perspective, it is extremely important, especially for a pastor doing spiritual direction, to disallow his human will to come between the true grace and will of God when ministering or helping others. A pastor should always be earnest in listening to the subtle mysteries and grace of God, and allow God's sometimes subtle message to infuse the pastor's rendering of spiritual direction, to be truly inspired rather than simply rely on one's worldly intellect and reading.

Peterson went on to describe the differences between some pastors, during his encounters as a youth growing up, and also when he was a young pastor. Some pastors engaged actively in worldly conversation with their congregational members, while others, only engaged in conversation that related to anything biblical or spiritual. In Peterson's interpretation in the chapter "The Ministry of Small Talk" (ibid, 111), he believed that since most ordinary people's lives have only a small percentage of spirituality, to engage only in spiritual conversation would divorce or distance the pastor from the congregation, without an active context for conversation, or involvement in the congregational members' lives. He also saw in himself, and some peers, who became impatient or apprehensive of "small talk", sometimes some pastors even veering towards arrogance, preferring instead to engage only in evangelistic talks of gospel. He felt this could be a shortcoming, as ordinary people would then also keep a safe distance from their pastors, and in so, have little reason to engage their pastors in spiritual direction. And through that distancing, the lack of spiritual direction and involvement between the pastors and the congregation may ultimately result in the decaying of spiritual communion with God, and the church, with the congregational members. Peterson suggested that pastors begin to cultivate conversational humility, by being down-to-earth and close to the ground with people. Peterson believed that the Holy Spirit is always present beforehand; in such "small talk" with the congregation, and that pastors can rely on and relinquish their egos to allow the grace of God through the work of the Holy Spirit, to keep the "small talk" alive. In so doing, pastors will become closer to the congregational members, and in return, a trust begins to build up from the congregational members, who will then trust the work and spiritual direction of the pastors, in helping the members grow closer to God.

Who are sinners? And how should pastors view the concept of sin and sinners? Peterson questioned this archaic topic in the chapter "Unwell in a New Way" (ibid, 117). Sometimes, he surmised that some pastors might begin to merge the concept of sin and sinners into a judgmental fashion. In Peterson's words,

> *"The word sinner is a theological designation. It is essential to insist on this. It is not a moralistic judgment"* (ibid, 118).

Therefore, it is important for pastors to view the concept of "sinners" merely as a state of divorce between man and God, which has nothing to do with the state of the people pastors meet. Such people can be extremely nice, pious, spiritual, charitable, and compassionate (or they can be anywhere from that to the other extreme). Still, it does not matter, or it should not matter, to the pastor rendering spiritual direction to help someone grow closer to God. Peterson reminded pastors that judgment is reserved for God and by God. By wrongfully merging the concept of "sinners" with people, may cause the pastors to breed resentment to ordinary people, and cause a rift from his own congregational members, and therefore render him useless to the service of God.

At the same time, pastors are sinners in the theological designation too, and some pastors lapse into a feeling of inadequacy, when ministering to his or her congregation. To this, Peterson uses Ephesians 1:15-16[19] as a method to address this feeling of inadequacy,

> *Paul says: "Wherefore I also, having heard of the faith in the Lord Jesus which is in you, and the love which ye have towards all the saints, do not cease giving thanks for you, making mention of you at my prayers..."*

Apostle Paul saw grace of God in every action of every man, and in so doing, was able to appreciate that while all people are sinners, he could see the grace of God working through these people's lives.

In the chapter "Lashed to the Mast" (ibid, 129), Peterson examined the constant tension and tussle between congregational members' expectations of a pastor, and the pastor's own vows as an ordained minister. Peterson used the analogy of a physician who would not bend under any pressure from his client, but rather stick to his own expertise diagnosis, and will only administer treatment in accordance with his expertise and diagnosis, as well as the Hippocratic Oath he took as a physician. Likewise, Peterson asserted that even under extreme pressure from the congregation to cave in to some mundane or worldly request that would run contrary to Word and sacrament, a pastor must resist the temptation to cave in and submit to the desires of the congregation, simply because that would ruin his ministry forever, and also allow the devil to work his craft on the congregation and the church. Therefore, Peterson urged pastors to always be steadfast in the observance of Word and sacrament, akin to being tied to a mast on a ship.

Pastors served in this calling based on a presumption of a lifetime of service to God's work. Therefore, it is very likely

---

[19] John Nelson Darby, Darby Bible - a literal translation of the Old Testament (1890) and the New Testament (1884). Public Domain - Copy Freely.

most pastors will serve a long time. However, as with any service or vocation, there is a human tendency to fatigue. To some, fatigue comes soon enough. For others, it may come a long time later. For Peterson, as he detailed in the chapter "Desert and Harvest: A Sabbatical Story" (ibid, 141), he saw the need for a sabbatical[20] after a long time serving his church Christ Our King Presbyterian Church, to recharge and remove the fatigue.

In Peterson's fashion, he described the sabbatical leave as "desert time", while the time spent on pastoral work or spiritual direction, as "harvest time". Much as we like to harvest as often or as consistently as we like, we must also allow the fields to take a break from growing crops, or "desert time". For Peterson, a prolific author, he took the sabbatical leave in order to learn from other pastors in other churches, and to have quiet time to concentrate on writing books. To him, time away after a long term ministry, especially to learn from other pastors, was necessary to allow him to find new perspectives, new delivery of sermons, and sometimes, new contemplation of the Bible.

For pastors, especially those who wish to stay with the same congregation as Peterson did for nearly three decades, the sabbatical must be well planned in advance, and well communicated to the congregation so that the members can understand and can happily support. In Peterson's case, he also advocated the use of a consistent "device" to engage his congregation, through the use of a monthly "Sabbatical Letter", during his year-long sabbatical, so that his congregation can stay in touch through Peterson's spiritual journey and progress away from them.

In the closing chapters "The Word Made Fresh" (ibid, 155), Peterson summoned his poetic side, to express many

---

[20]Sabbatical commonly refers to a leave of absence from work for research, study, or simply travel, usually associated with academics.

of his thoughts that biblical prophets and psalmists were all poets, and so he wrote several poems in praise of his life and ministry in the service of God. Of course, being a good pastor in the service of God's work on earth, does not necessarily mandate the use of poetry, although it is certainly powerful and contemplative. For the congregation leading hurried lives, it would sometimes be harder to be able to digest and assimilate the subtle wisdom encased within the short verses of poems. Peterson's gift of being to express in poetry perhaps is also a subtle and gentle reminder to pastors, that pastoral work and spiritual direction can take many forms, and expressed through God's grace in many forms.

Top 5 Themes and Why

Peterson's premise of a pastor perceived by ordinary people as a benign and yet often "brushed-aside" entity, served as a powerful wake-up call that pastors cannot simply deliver sermons and become sidelined by the congregation in the rest of the days of the week of the livelihoods of the congregational members.

Second, Peterson's advice of seeking to be "unbusy", to be able to blend in the secular lives of the ordinary folks by being a "subversive", and taking on an "apocalyptic" cloak can be methodical ways to refine pastoral work and spiritual direction.

Third, the chapter on "Praying with Eyes Open" seemed to remind pastors that sometimes we have to "stop and smell the roses", to appreciate God's creation, to realize that God's grace exist and manifest in many subtle forms, and that a brisk walk, a busy day, or simply nonchalance, may sometimes turn pastors blind to such grace. Appreciating such grace may indeed strengthen a pastor in his ministry and spiritual direction. This important theme perhaps shares some connection with a later chapter on the need for a pastor to sometimes take a sabbatical away from ministry, to be able to recharge himself or herself for further growth with a communion with God, and a better closeness with the congregational members.

Fourth, Peterson asserted that a pastor may have to grow in the use of a language of love and prayer in order to help the congregational members to grow in their relationship with God, rather than using prescriptive or motivational language only, in the chapter "First Language".

Lastly, in the chapter "Unwell in a New Way", Peterson reminded pastors to see the concepts of "sinners" as a theological designation, rather than pass judgment on congregational members, so as to grow universal love and compassion for the congregation, rather than resentment.

Author's Notes

The author believes that this book by Peterson serves a full palette of tools and wisdom for a practicing pastor, especially one serving in geographies steeped in diverse beliefs, philosophies, and customs that in many circumstances create great challenges compared to a more homogenous landscape where Christianity is more prevalent. This book provides a balanced and contemplative thinking that allows pastors to exercise more love and compassion when rendering spiritual direction, especially useful in difficult circumstances, whether in people or areas where Christian theology may be challenged to a great extent, or even objected to.

Early Christian Thought

Early Christian Thought

Abstract

Reverend Robert Louis Wilken has eloquently written a book that serves to educate not only peers, but also the everyday Christian, in his book "The Spirit of Early Christian Thought".

Wilken's book is broken down into four parts – foundations, teachings, the believers, the cultural context of Christianity, and principles of discipleship.

The chapters on foundations dealt with the early knowledge of God, of prayer and sacraments, and the emergence of the Bible, as we know today. The following chapters on teachings discussed the Triune God, which is definitive of Christianity, what Jesus Christ did, how orthodox Christianity view creation of the world, and the place of human beings in this world. The next two chapters on believers discussed the important concept of salvation through the primacy by faith[21], and that of the fellowship within the universal church of believers to strengthen God's kingdom on earth. The next two chapters of the book dealt with the cultural aspects of Christianity in regards to poetry, symbols, and objects, and can be important in establishing some of our contemporary understanding behind the physical manifestations of various mainstream denominations of Catholicism, Orthodox Church, and the Protestant denominations. The next chapters discussed on how to lead a moral and spiritual life as a Christian disciple, which often can be grounds for contemporary and ongoing debates within some denominations, on what makes a good Christian. Views may vary, but the key learning point from these chapters are really about how to lead a spiritually charged and inspired life.

---

[21] Salvation by faith alone (Latin: Sola fides), or justification by faith alone, is one of the hallmark characteristics of the Protestant movement, based on Dr Martin Luther's challenge to the Roman Catholic Church and its practice of granting indulges (Wikipedia, 2007).

In Chapter 1 "Founded on the Cross of Christ" (Wilken, 2003, 1), Reverend Wilken discussed the split between the fundamental theology of the Christians and Judaism, then both followed by Jews. The split occurred when Christians viewed Jesus Christ as our true and only Messiah, while fellow Jews in those times, did not. In the chapter, Wilken showed that early Christian thinking did not attempt to establish the church in the same enthusiasm as we do today in church planting and the evangelism of the Gospel. Rather, in the early Christian times, it would appear that it was more about understanding and explaining the theology itself, especially to skeptics, critics, and even believers. The early Christian thinkers were apologists[22], who bravely debated and fought off skepticism and even persecution. One such early apologist was Justin Martyr (ibid, 4), who was first a Greek philosopher, before becoming a Christian. Martyr experienced the difference between Plato's ways as a philosopher, a reliance on demonstration, to that of a witness (based on lives of prophets, who have seen and experienced personal events). Martyr also stressed the importance of affections, that of a Christian's way to love God with "all your heart and with all your soul and with all your might".

Another philosopher, which till today can be seen in some controversy, is Origen[23] of Alexandria, who wrote "Against Celsus" (Latin: Contra Celsum), to dispute against the anti-Christian second century Greek philosopher

---

[22] Apologists (derived from the Greek word "apologia"), were people who defended a position or thought against attacks (Wikipedia, 2007).
[23] Origen of Alexandria was an early Christian theologian and was controversial in many ways, although his works also helped shape Christianity later on. (Wikipedia, 2007) (New Advent Catholic Encyclopedia, Internet, 2007).

Celsus[24]. Origen also wrote about the elect people of God, the Jews, who followed their way of life based on revelation of the Law to Moses. Christians however, recognized the concept of God's grace, since only God can bestow the ability to allow humans, as sinners, to know God, as shown in the case of how Abraham (ibid, 19) experience God only because God allowed Himself to be experienced by Abraham, a act of God's grace.

While some may contest that Christianity seem to place faith above reason, Wilken reasoned that past Christian theologians and saints, were people of reason. For example, Saint Augustine[25] of Hippo wrote "anyone who supposes that the senses are never to be trusted in woefully mistaken" (ibid, 23), or Saint John of Damascus[26], who said, "the mind which is determined to ignore corporeal things will find itself weakened and frustrated".

In chapter 2 "An Awesome and Unbloody Sacrifice" (ibid, 25), Wilken starts by exalting that a true Christian theologian must be one who prays diligently, quoting the desert monk Evagrius "A theologian is one who prays, and one who prays is a theologian" (ibid, 26). Therefore, the foundation of an orthodox Christian should center around worship, and not simply in philosophy. Worship and prayer take many forms, and Wilken then discussed how Origen and many others cited the importance of Christian worship

---

[24] Celsus, the second century Greek philosopher wrote the book "The True Word", which later Christian theologian Origen disputed inn his apologetic work "Against Celsus".

[25] Saint Augustine of Hippo, or Aurelius Augustinus (354-430 AD) was considered one of the early "church fathers", and is venerated as a saint of both the Roman Catholic Church and the Anglican Communion (Wikipedia, 2007).

[26] Saint John of Damascus (676-749 AD) is venerated especially by the Eastern Orthodox Church as an apologist, theologian, and poet (Wikipedia, 2007) (Catholic.org, Internet, 2007).

through baptism, and the Eucharist, which not only celebrates the presence of the living Christ, but also affirm the Triune God.

Unlike modern practices of baptism, which have largely dispensed with many liturgical components in preference to a simpler form, the early Christian forms of baptism were much more elaborate (ibid, 39). But in the entire lineage of baptism practice, it is obvious that water is symbolic of sanctification of a person, and it showed through the various stages of Christ's life that His life was too, linked to water, through his baptism, his inaugurating of a marriage, when preaching, his miracle of walking on water, and even right up to his passion (ibid, 41).

The Eucharist is also discussed at some length. Wilken mentioned that while outsiders can see the Eucharist as a "ceremony", it is much more spiritually charged than that, in that it celebrates the divine mysteries. Beyond the reading of memoirs and writings during the Eucharist, the presiding minister would often also urge the congregation to follow through those noble concepts and practices. The Eucharist also celebrates the faithful departed, and counts them among us in the grace of God. In the Roman Catholic and Orthodox traditions, the Eucharist may have different meanings and expression compared to Protestant denominations, but the spirit of the Eucharist is universally shared, that of a noble and faithful expression of a love and celebration for the Triune God.

In Chapter 3 "The Face of God for Now" (ibid, 50), Wilken asserted the importance of the Bible in Christian discipleship, by opening with Saint Augustine's words, "For now treat the Script of God as the face of God. Melt in its presence." It is indeed true for contemporary Christians, having no direct connection with ancient history or any links to oral teachings by lineage, the Bible becomes the only inerrant scepter that holds all that we know about God, and in embracing the orthodox Christian life.

According to Wilken, one of the best examples of how someone could fathom and marvel at the Bible was Greek philosopher and theologian Clement of Alexandria[27]. Clement of Alexandria was different from other Christian theologians, in that he was not a bishop, but a layman, and being grounded previously in secular philosophy, made his writings decidedly different. Therefore, although Clement of Alexandria was venerated as a saint in the seventeenth century, his name was dropped subsequently by Pope Clement VIII, on the grounds that Clement's writings, although Christian inspired, also talked extensively on the concept of "gnosis"[28], which is part of Gnosticism[29], or Christian mysticism, and so his thinking was estranged from the mainstream Christianity, and did not get much consideration thereafter. In the book, Wilken did stress on Clement's contributions in terms of melding the thinking and logic of Plato, into interpreting the Bible. Wilken then went on to describe the emergence of the Old Testament (otherwise known as the Jewish Bible), and New Testament (from the apostolic writings), and also, the Apocrypha, works which the Protestants no longer study which is

---

[27] Clement of Alexandria (birth unknown, died between 211 to 216), was a Greek philosopher and later Christian theologian, who melded Greek thinking with Christian doctrine, in a systematic and scientific way (Wikipedia, 2007) (Catholic Encyclopedia, Internet, 2007).

[28] Gnosis is the Greek word for knowledge, which in today's context is taken to mean experiential knowledge of the spiritual mysteries (Wikipedia, 2007).

[29] Gnosticism is a diverse spiritual movement that talks about an imperfect deity and a mostly unknown supreme being. Some Gnostics (otherwise known as Christian Gnostics, believe that Jesus Christ came to teach an esoteric knowledge that only the elite would know. Other Gnostics can include the likes of Vajrayana Buddhists (found in Tibet, Nepal and some parts of India), which stress on rather esoteric rituals, meditations, and scriptures (Wikipedia, 2007).

included within the Catholic Bible, such as the books of the Maccabees and the Wisdom of Solomon (ibid, 62).

Another key figure in the early church development was Irenaeus[30], exalted as saint in the Catholic and Eastern Orthodox traditions, and considered as the "father of the church". Irenaeus was consecrated as bishop of Lugdunum in Gaul, and his writings were foundations of many of contemporary Christian theology. One of his famous summaries read:

> *This, then, is the ordering of our faith... God, the Father, uncreated, incomprehensible, invisible, one God, creator of all.... (ibid, 65)*

Irenaeus' summary became the Apostles' Creed used in many Christian rites today, which now reads:

> *"I believe in God, the Father almighty, creator of heaven and earth. I believe in Jesus Christ, God's only Son, our Lord, who was conceived by the Holy Spirit, born of the Virgin Mary, suffered under Pontius Pilate, was crucified, died, and was buried; he descended to the dead. On the third day he rose again; he ascended into heaven, he is seated at the right hand of the Father, and he will come to judge the living and the dead. I believe in the Holy Spirit, the holy catholic Church, the communion of saints, the forgiveness of sins, the resurrection of the body, and the life everlasting. Amen." (Ecumenical version).*

Wilken then went on to discuss the concept of allegory, or spiritual and deeper interpretations of the Bible. For example, Origen believed that Paul interpreted the Exodus

---

[30] Irenaeus (born second century, died end of third or beginning of third century), was bishop of Lugdunum in Gaul, now Lyon in France. His classical and defining work was Adversus Haereses (Against Heresies) (Wikipedia, 2007).

and the wandering of the Jews in the desert, differently from the plain words of the writings. While Jews simply called it the crossing of the sea, Paul called it baptism. While the Jews talked about a cloud, Paul called it the coming of the Holy Spirit. Therefore, Wilken concluded that the Bible has many layers of meanings, each deeper and more profound than the last. This perhaps serves to allow Christians of various intellect and stage of learning, to be able to get as much of God's Word as he or she can assimilate, and as the Christian grows in faith and understanding with God's grace, will be able to decipher and uncover more and more of the Bible's profound wisdom. However, the deeper interpretation of the Bible requires a clear-headed understanding of the context surrounding the text. All too often, some Christians, and sometimes even ministers, interpret the Bible erroneously, when the holistic context of the passage, was not properly considered and studied. It is easy to simply attach a meaning to a single sentence, while ignoring the larger context of the whole passage. This is what Wilken warned about when interpreting the Bible. The chapter closes with Wilken having described how Gregory the Great (ibid, 77) lived the life according to the Bible. It is insufficient to simply read the Bible, or even understand it intellectually. To be a true Christian, one must live and embrace the Bible.

In Chapter 4 "Seek His Face Always", Wilken discussed the concept of the Triune God, which went against the older Judaism, and presented challenges to early Church leaders. Origen had a dialog with Arabian bishop Heraclides, in the work "Dialog with Heraclides", to pin down the concept of the Triune God, especially in the concept of the Father and of the Son. Eventually, that led to the meeting of bishops at Nicaea, known as the First Council of Nicaea (325 AD), with a creed later known as the Nicene Creed (usually quoted along with the Apostles'

Creed for articles of faith) (Wikipedia, 2007), an ecumenical Christian statement of faith usually accepted by all mainstream Roman Catholic, Eastern Orthodox and Protestant traditions:

> *"We believe in one God, the Father, the Almighty, maker of heaven and earth, of all that is, seen and unseen. We believe in one Lord, Jesus Christ, the only Son of God, eternally begotten of the Father, God from God, Light from Light, true God from true God, begotten, not made, of one Being with the Father; through him all things were made. For us and for our salvation he came down from heaven, was incarnate of the Holy Spirit and the Virgin Mary and became truly human. For our sake he was crucified under Pontius Pilate; he suffered death and was buried. On the third day he rose again in accordance with the Scriptures; he ascended into heaven and is seated at the right hand of the Father. He will come again in glory to judge the living and the dead, and his kingdom will have no end. We believe in the Holy Spirit, the Lord, the giver of life, who proceeds from the Father and the Son, who with the Father and the Son is worshiped and glorified, who has spoken through the prophets. We believe in one holy catholic and apostolic Church. We acknowledge one baptism for the forgiveness of sins. We look for the resurrection of the dead, and the life of the world to come. Amen."*

Hilary of Poitieres (ibid, 86) was able to demonstrate that Christ's Resurrection brought about the transformation of early Jews to see that God was able to come as Christ the Son, such as when Thomas proclaimed "My Lord and my God!" when he saw the risen Christ. The recognition of the Holy Spirit came later, especially in the eventual celebration of the Pentecost. The main manifestation of the emergence of the Holy Spirit must be the Eucharist, where the bishop would proclaim (ibid, 101):

> "We pray that You would send Your Holy Spirit upon the offerings of Your holy church; that gathering them into one, You would grant to all your saints who partake of them to be filled with the Holy Spirit."

Likewise, when a bishop is consecrated, the Holy Spirit is again mentioned (ibid, 101):

> "Pour forth now that power which is Yours of Your royal Spirit which You gave to Your beloved servant Jesus Christ which He bestowed on His holy apostles... And by the Spirit of high-priesthood give him authority to remit sins according to Your commandments."

Wilken put it in a very understandable manner with regards to the Holy Spirit (ibid, 102):

> Rather every divine action that has to do with creation and is designated according to our different conceptions has its origin in the Father, passes through the Son, and is brought to completion by the Holy Spirit.

One of the key works on the Triune God was written by Saint Augustine[31], known as "De Trinitate" (The Trinity), a long and complex work that explained his understanding of the Triune God. But most important short phrase in his work had to be "Seek His face always", not only in intellectual and theological understanding, but one of seeking God to love Him and honor Him.

In Chapter 5 "Not My Will But Thine" (ibid 110), Wilken described early Christina thinkers often engaging in debate, which in a sense, is a necessary step to understand the collective thinking better, so that the church eventually

---

[31] Saint Augustine of Hippo, or Aurelius Augustinus, was an early Church father venerated by the Roman Catholic Church (Stanford Encyclopedia of Philosophy, Internet, 2007).

can minister more effectively to the people. But Christian history is fraught with many debates and struggles, and for example, there were successive councils of attempting to resolve theological disputes, such as the council of Nicaea in 325 AD, the council of Constantinople in 381 AD, the council of Ephesus in 431, Chalcedon in 451 AD, Constantinople II in 553 AD, and so on.

One of the key debates was the divinity of Jesus Christ. The docetists believed that Christ only seemed human. The Ebionites denied Christ as divine but just a noble human sage, while the mainstream Christian traditions maintained that Christ was fully divine and fully human. Another sticking point was Virgin Mary as mother of Christ, which started as a major debate between Nestorius, bishop of Constantinople and Cyril, bishop of Alexandria, in the fifth century (ibid, 115).

Cyril wrote extensively on the divinity of Christ, and one of his key explanations by using the Resurrection of Christ, which appealed to the people in a powerful and yet easy to understand manner (ibid, 121):

"If he (Christ) conquered as God, to us it is nothing; but if he conquered as man we conquered in Him. For he is to us the second Adam come from heaven according to the Scriptures."

One of the key characters in this chapter, was Maximus the Confessor[32]. Maximus rooted for the position that for Jesus Christ to be fully divine and also fully human, He had

---

[32] Maximus the Confessor, or Saint Maximus of Constantinople, is known as the "Theologian", in the Roman Catholic Church. He was against the position of Monothelitism (one will of Christ), and proclaimed that Christ has both a divine and human will. For that, he was exiled, mutilated, and subsequently died in exile. He was venerated as a saint soon after his death (Wikipedia, 2007) (Catholic Encyclopedia, Internet, 2007).

to have both a divine will, and a human will. He illustrated this by an example in Matthew 26:39, when Christ said, "Father, if it be possible, let the cup pass from me", exhibiting Christ's human will. And yet, Maximus also explained that Christ did not have an antagonistic human will against divine will, but both will that work in tandem, in that the human will of Christ was deified. The Emperor in Constantinople saw this view as heresy and he issued a decree "Typos", which would punish anyone who proclaimed the concept of two wills of Christ. The Roman Pope Martin also rooted for the same position, and subsequently was publicly humiliated and later died from starvation, cold, and mistreatment (ibid, 134). Maximus suffered an even worse fate than Pope Martin, with his right hand cut off, tongue ripped out, and exiled to Caucasus, and subsequently died there.

In Chapter 6 "The End Given in the Beginning" (ibid 136), Wilken discussed the concept of God's creations, which in Genesis of the Bible, is powerful and yet controversial against many other faiths or cultures. As it was said in the Bible, "In the beginning God created the heaven and the earth", which Wilken took it to mean that Christianity has displaced cosmology and ruled out human hypotheses on random and disordered formation of the known universe. What's more profound to Saint Gregory[33], was that God created man in His image and likeness. However, what separates humans from God, is sin.

In Chapter 7 "The Reasonableness of Faith" (ibid, 162), Wilken discussed one of the key criticisms of

---

[33] Gregory of Nazianzus (329 - 389 AD), was a fourth century Christian bishop of Constantinople, not to be confused with Saint Gregory the Great (Pope Gregory I). Gregory was most remembered as the theologian who explained the Trinitarian principles. His elder brother, Basil the Great, and Gregory, were both exalted as saints and founding fathers of theology (Wikipedia, 2007).

Christianity, especially when faced with would-be believers and cynics, that of simply having faith before reason, as in "If you believe you will understand" (Isaiah 7:9).

Wilken illustrated through the historical example of how Saint Augustine explained the concept of faith in some detail. Wilken mentioned that when Augustine was advocating faith, he was not talking about blind allegiance or simplistic submission to authority. Rather, Augustine meant that one can place confidence in people he or she love or admire, and follow the examples lived out by such people. Therefore, it is clearly easy to follow the path of a Christian life, because it is agreeable that Jesus led a wondrous and admired life, and one that justifies faith.

Wilken also illustrated with the example of Saint John (ibid, 177) who saw the physical body of Jesus Christ, and yet his words seemed to imply a whole lot more, that he saw "life" in Christ. So although Christ took a human form, it must be apparent to someone like Saint John to be able to see beyond the mere human form of Christ, to bear witness to something greater, to see more, as Wilken put it, the "Word of God". It also implied that not everyone has the innate ability to sense, to see, or to hear God, even as God presents Himself in front of someone. Jesus Christ said, "Let him who has ears to hear, hear" (Matthew 11:15). One must possess the prerequisite faith in order to sense God, and to embrace the relationship with Him, in order to know Him. Also, someone with the ability and the desire to sense and relate to God personally, tend to take on the form of a witness (ibid, 181). Wilken made an observation that unlike a journalist, who usually reports from the third person and detached perspective, a Christian witness often relates experiences in the first person and involved perspective.

In Chapter 8 "Happy the People Whose God Is the Lord" (ibid, 186), Wilken outlined Saint Augustine's colossal writing, "The City of God", which took Augustine over fifteen years to complete, with the last book being completed in 426 AD when Augustine was in his seventies. What "The City of God" stood for was not theology, but more of Augustine's need to show the importance of the universal church of God in relation to Christians and their living in the Word of God, within the earthly and mundane confines of daily life. Augustine wanted to demonstrate that while Christians live a Christ-inspired righteous life and seek eternal life and salvation through Christ, there is still a temporal and earthly life that must be fulfilled, in the best possible ways in God's honor.

Wilken also illustrated how Augustine, through his work "The City of God", showed that every Christian has a role to play in the temporal world. Not everyone is suited or elected by God to enter monastic service or to denounce worldly duties. Augustine's close friend general Boniface (ibid, 201), a staunch Catholic, wanted to give up military duties and become a monastic monk when his wife died while they were stationed in Africa. Instead of encouraging Boniface, Augustine urged him to continue to serve Rome as a general. Augustine explained that Boniface needed to protect and serve the community. So Augustine's key point was that while every Christian should have a dedicated lifetime of prayer, not everyone can live by prayer alone (as a monk). Many would need to fulfill earthly duties, where every one of these duties serve God's purpose and kingdom on earth in some way. This chapter was gratifying that while some people yearn for a secluded religious life, the real faith is often tested and proven out in the real world, where experiences and challenges are confronted, solved, and new wisdom through God's irresistible grace, are revealed.

In Chapter 9 "The Glorious Deeds of Christ" (ibid, 212), Wilken illustrated the poetry of the Christian faith, where witnesses wrote about their faith and their exaltations in Christ and God, through a variety of biblically-styled poetry, prose, and hymns. Much of the poetry of early Christian writers were written in more classical languages and grammar, and would appeal especially to the literate, and the studied, in the contemporary world.

The first Christian poet to achieve success with the people was Ambrose, bishop of Milan in the fourth century (ibid, 217), who could be considered as one of the most admired liturgical poets of all time. Some of his hymns used the iambic dimeter[34], such as this opening stanza in Latin (with a translated English version right after) (ibid, 219):

> *Splendor paternae gloriae du luce lucem proferens lux lucis et fons luminis diem dies inluminans.*
>
> *O Jesus, Lord of heavenly grace, Thou brightness of thy Father's face, Thou fountain of eternal light, Whose beams disperse the shades of night.*

Another poet during the time was Prudentius[35], a contemporary of Ambrose. However, Prudentius was not a liturgical poet like Ambrose whose poems and hymns are to be recited or sung in church during service. Rather, Prudentius' poetry was meant to be read in personal space, and contemplated upon.

In Chapter 10 "Making This Thing Other" (ibid, 237), Wilken started with the view that many critics of Christianity despised Christianity for a simple practice, that of venerating the dead. However, he shared the view with

---

[34] Iambic dimeter (ibid, 219) is an iambic foot of short/long in a line of two equal parts. Each line has eight syllables, each stanza has four lines, and all hymns contain eight stanzas. The word "iambic" or "iamb" is a metrical foot in poetry, which started in Greek as in "i-amb", for a short syllable followed by a long syllable (Wikipedia, 2007).

[35] Aurelius Prudentius Clemens (born 348 AD, died probably 413 AD), or simply Prudentius, was a Roman Christian poet (Wikipedia, 2007).

many great Christian thinkers such as Gregory of Nyssa, Saint Basil and Cyril of Alexandria, that what was observed in the physical form was often much more than just a physical and dead object, but could be an expression of Christian mystery, and could help many pious Christians bond stronger with their faith in God. For example, Gregory of Nyssa chided Eunomius for ignoring Christian practices and focused only on theology. To Gregory, the Eucharist, with its physical expressions of using bread and wine, or the sign of the Cross when reciting the phrase "The Father, Son, and Holy Spirit", are sacramental and should not be discarded as mere rituals (ibid 239). In this chapter, Wilken attempted to show that many physical and worldly things, when imbued with a Christ-centric thought, can take on an "other" form or emerge as a new phenomenon.

The emergence of Christian art, and especially the expressions of Christ in physical form, was also a matter of grave debate in the early years. For it was said in the Old Testament, where the law of Moses said, "Thou shalt not make thyself any graven image, or any form of what is in the heavens above, or what is in the earth beneath, or what is in the waters under the earth" (Exodus 20:4-5). John of Damascus[36] saw things quite differently. To John, God worked out salvations of people through matter, and that matter can be filled with God's grace and power, and in turn, inspire Christians. John said (ibid, 248):

> "I treat all matter with reverence and respect, because it is filled with divine grace and power".

Physical representations of Christ, such as paintings found at the Monastery of Saint Catherine at Mount Sinai

---

[36] John of Damascus (676 -749 AD), was a Syrian monk and presbyter who wrote "Fountain of Knowledge", as well as three "Apologetic Treatises against those Decrying the Holy Images" (Wikipedia, 2007).

(ibid, 247), was the church's way to show that God appeared in human flesh, through a historically real person of Jesus Christ. In 692 AD, the synod in Constantinople decreed (ibid, 253):

> "In order to bring this reality before the eyes of everyone in an image, we decree that from now on the human likeness of Christ our God, the lam who takes away the sins of the world, should be painted on icons, in place of the ancient lamb. In this way we will grasp the depth of humility of the Word of God, and will be prompted to remember his life in the flesh, his suffering, his salvific death, and the salvation that has come to the world."

The reality is that humans usually find it more difficult to deal with abstract concepts or entities, and tend to identify with some form of sensory reality. Still, it must be remembered that the physical signs and images only serve as reminders of the deeds of Christ and serve only as markers for reverence.

In Chapter 11 "Likeness to God" (ibid, 262), Wilken started by saying that humans tend to require examples to follow, or imitate. The author often remembers in his youth, his first education in Chinese calligraphy and ink painting, was to first diligently copy known masterpieces, time after time. Only by copying the masterpieces diligently and consistently, a young painter can learn the basics, and then attempt to go on to learn flair and personal expression. Likewise, a Christian has the Bible, full of highly inspiring examples of people who led Spirit-filled lives, and walked the path of purity, wisdom, and faith. The best example to attempt to humbly follow, must surely be our Lord Jesus Christ.

A structured program for spiritual direction, can be found in the works of Saint Ignatius Loyola[37], founder of the Society of Jesus[38]. Loyola's works provided a system with moral exercises, good habits formation, self-examination, contemplation on edifying sayings, of noble examples, under the tutelage of a master (ibid, 268).

But the most defining work on not only attaining moral authority, but more than that, to attain holiness and true happiness, was the Beatitudes (which in Latin "beatitudo" means happiness). In the Beatitudes (Matthew 5:3-12), Jesus described the qualities for the citizens of the Kingdom of heaven, and explained what it meant to be truly blessed and enjoy fellowship with God. For example, Jesus said, "Blessed are the pure in heart for they shall see God".

In Galatians 5:22-23[39], Paul wrote:

> "But the fruit of the Spirit is love, joy, peace, long-suffering, kindness, goodness, fidelity, meekness, self-control: against such things there is no law." (Darby, 1889).

Beyond morality and then holiness, the ultimate expression of these cardinal virtues should be the expression of love for God (ibid, 286), which is in turn the filling of our hearts by the Holy Spirit. This again shows the irresistible grace God extends to His children.

---

[37] Saint Ignatius of Loyola (1491-1556 AD), was the founder of the Society of Jesus, and the followers were known as the Jesuits (Wikipedia, 2007).

[38] The Society of Jesus is a Catholic Order, whose motto is "Iesus Homini Salvator" which stands for "Jesus, Savior of Mankind". They were also known to be "counter-reformers" of the Roman Catholic Church, to counter the reformation brought about by Protestantism (Wikipedia, 2007) (Catholic Encyclopedia, Internet, 2007).

[39] Wilken quoted Galatians 5:16 for the inline quoted passage, which should be 5:22-23.

In Chapter 12 "The Knowledge of Sensuous Intelligence" (ibid, 291), Wilken discussed the seemingly polarized attributes of a faithful Christian. On one hand, determined and consistent self-discipline away from the sins is mandatory. On the other, a flourishing expression of love and passion for God and His Word is also necessary. Discipline often has to do with the turning away of emotional upheaval, such as the expression of anger and hate. And yet, the flip side of anger and hate is love. But there is no paradox in the Bible. Where the expression of love and desire is directed by the Holy Spirit in honor of God, it is rooted in good. When the expression of love and desire is directed by evil thoughts or unruly passions, it is rooted in evil (ibid, 304).

Finally, Wilken ended his book with an Epilogue (ibid, 312), which he summarized that early Christian thinkers were trying to unite Christian thinking when they wrote their treatises, books and even poems. The early thinkers were not merely attempting to be intellectuals or scholars, but were trying very hard to put a right perspective to help people understand God's Word better, or doctrinally more accurately. While some were apologetic in nature, most were simply passionate works of faith to help inspire believers of their time. Wilken aptly described that thought the early Christian thinkers were in a long gone era, their works still continue to inspire and teach us today.

Top 5 Themes and Why

Wilken's book contained many intertwined themes and descriptions, which could be complex and demanded much more reading outside the book, in order to understand the context of the book in relation to God's Word.

Evagrius who said, "A theologian is one who prays, and one who prays is a theologian" (ibid, 26), was exceptionally important to new and experienced ministers alike, since sometimes a pastor may minister and preach often, but not pray often enough. The saying was a strong reminder for the author to ensure that study and prayer must be done always.

Saint Augustine said, "For now treat the Script of God as the face of God. Melt in its presence" (ibid, 50). Those words reminded the author that at the root of everything in practice and preaching, always return to the Word of God as the source of wisdom.

Third, the Apostles' Creed and the Nicene Creed are useful markers to always affirm the fundamental principles an orthodox Christian should adhere to.

Fourth, the author was reminded of the importance of the Holy Spirit, especially in the reminder of his own ordination, and his personal experiences in his journey.

Lastly, the concept of faith before reason, and in turn, God's opening of our eyes to learn of His Word and wisdom, through a fellowship with Him, was exceptionally important to the author, again to remind him that while the intellectual study of Christian thought is important, he must always ensure that faith takes precedence.

Author's Notes

While many may prefer contemporary lingo, language, and life stories, there would be instances where a pastor would be questioned on the early Christian thought, especially on the formative thoughts that helped shape some of the modern Christian thinking. Wilken's work serves as a concise condensation of many of these early Christian thoughts and their writers, so that the author can help paint a more continuous imagery for his congregation.

Mere Christianity by CS Lewis

CS Lewis and Mere Christianity

Abstract

Saint Augustine said, "In essentials, unity. In nonessentials, liberty. In all things, charity". Perhaps Clive Staples Lewis, or better known as C. S. Lewis, was guided by this principle when he wrote the book "Mere Christianity". Lewis attempted to explain Christianity to other lay people like him, by avoiding contested or controversial issues that in his view, were best left to philosophers, clergy, and theologians. After all, "Mere Christianity" started out as a series of BBC[40] radio talks Lewis gave to soldiers at the battlefront, between 1942 to 1944, to bring solace and peace to the soldiers, many of whom are young and inexperienced, fighting what was to become one of the epic wars – the Second World War. Lewis talked about creation and human nature, the emergence of God, Christian morality and the concept of holiness as behavior, and some basics of Christian theology. Throughout the book, he avoided denominational and sectarian differences, as well as difficult issues such as birth control, because he admitted that was best left to theologians and ordained ministers, and also because he believed in uniting Christians, rather than dividing them. Lewis, as a well-known children's book author, also exercised his favorite form of expression throughout the book, that of masterful story telling and a liberal use of analogy, to explain some of the concepts. Perhaps Lewis understood that radio talks must be engaging, and cannot be laden with heavy jargon or abstract concepts.

Clive Staples Lewis, or C. S. Lewis, is perhaps one of the best storytellers of our time. Many people are immediately familiar with the blockbuster movie "The

---

[40] BBC stands for British Broadcasting Corporation. BBC started out in 1922 as the British Broadcasting Company Limited, and gained Royal Charter and then became state-owned in 1927 (Wikipedia, 2007).

Chronicles of Narnia"[41], based on his series of seven fantasy storybooks of "The Chronicles of Narnia". Although the fantasy stories told of fantastic creatures and sorcery, Lewis, being a Christian apologist at that time, included Christian concepts into these stories. So while the Narnia books were meant for children, they told of good versus evil with some Christian undertones.

Even as most people seem to attach importance to Lewis' fictional novels, he was also a serious Christian writer, having been converted to Christian during his adulthood. "Mere Christianity" is just one of the many Christian-centric books he came to write about.

"Mere Christianity" was originally not a single book, but rather, a series of transcripts based on his on-air broadcasts with BBC Radio, circa 1942 to 1944, titled "The Case for Christianity", "Christian Behavior", and "Beyond Personality". Lewis took these transcripts and expanded them further, and eventually finishing the book "Mere Christianity". The book is basically Lewis' understanding of Christian ethics and behavior, written for a layperson just like him, without too many towering theological concepts, and far away from abstract ideas or controversial themes. Lewis himself asserted that being neither theologian nor ordained minister, he would much prefer not dwelling on more esoteric issues.

"Mere Christianity" is separated into four "books". In Book 1, Lewis talked about the "Right and Wrong as a Clue to the Meaning of the Universe" (chapters 1:1-5). In Book 2, Lewis talked about "What Christians Believe" (chapters 2:1-5). In Book 3, Lewis talked about "Christian behavior"

---

[41] "The Chronicles of Narnia", was the cinematic representation from Disney, of C. S. Lewis' series of seven books, also titled "The Chronicles of Narnia" (Narnia.com, Internet, 2007).

(chapters 3:1-12). In Book 4, Lewis talked about "Beyond Personality" (chapters 4:1-11).

In Book 1 (Lewis, 2001, 3), Lewis observed that there is a "Law of Nature", or rather, a "Law of Right and Wrong", which every human being seem to understand, and yet not quite completely conform to. He gave an example of an untrustworthy person who would go back on his promise, and yet when the same is done to him, he would utter, "It's not fair". Many other laws of nature govern us as human beings, which we cannot defy, such as the law of gravity which deny us the ability to simply float into the air at will. Therefore, Lewis asserted that while human beings have to adhere to common laws of nature, they are only able to defy the one rule of "Law of Right and Wrong", or that of morality.

Next, Lewis talked about objections from people who disputed the Moral Law or the law of human nature (ibid, 9), and his own observations. Lewis felt that the objections that Moral Law could be simply instinct or nurture through education (ibid, 12), could not quite explain why humans behave in certain norms, that of doing the "right" things. Lewis used one interesting argument, that if a person's house does not have mousetraps because the dweller believes there are no mice in the house, it does not mean he has a humane heart. Therefore, it might simply boil down to perception and belief, that would guide moral principles of a person, and that often, means a higher spiritually attuned heart that relies on a stronger foundation or mountain, such as faith on God.

Lewis further asserted that while many of us have preconceived notions (ibid, 16) about what good or socially acceptable behavior should be, it is really a case of hit-or-miss, since unlike laws of gravity and other well-defined laws of physics, what Lewis termed "law of human nature" does not necessarily bind all humans to behave in the same manner. So while a stone or a leaf both conform to the laws of gravity and will hit the ground, not every person will behave in the socially acceptable norms.

Lewis then questioned the concept of how our universe or even our earth came about (ibid, 21). Lewis went through some lengths to ask questions, if the universe simply existed, or came to exist, or there could be some greater power that fueled its formation. Lewis took it slowly to discuss the possibility of a greater power behind the direction of the universe. Lewis labeled the two views of the universe as the Materialist view (that of the universe that exist due to various non-supernatural reasons, such as the "big bang"[42]) and the Religious view (that of God creating and guiding the formation of the universe). Lewis then hinted that the supernatural entity behind the creation of the universe, especially since Lewis is a Christian apologist, namely God, cannot be an entity that creates the universe and then no longer interferes or manages its direction.

Lewis then explained that there must be a great deal of discomfort (ibid, 28), if we know that there is a greater supernatural force, such as God, which stands for universal goodness and righteousness. This is because humans have many failings, ranging from minor indiscretions, to major crimes such as murder, and any of these indiscretions or crimes must be seen as utterly disgusting in the presence of a completely righteous supernatural being, such as God, in Lewis' assertions.

In Book 2 (ibid, 35), Lewis began to explore and expound on the concepts and ideas behind what Christians

---

[42] The "big bang" is a cosmological model of the creation of the universe is whereby a tiny dense and highly heated matter expands over billions of years, to form the various galaxies and planetary systems (Wikipedia, 2007).

believe. Lewis first mentioned that there are more people who believed in some form of supernatural forces, than those who do not (atheists[43]). Lewis also mentioned there are two worldviews of God. There are Pantheists[44] who believe God is beyond good or evil, and IS the universe itself, which also means without the universe, the Pantheist version of God ceases to exist. There are also others (including Judaism, Christianity, and Islam), who believe that God must be completely righteous and good, and that God created the universe, and exists independently from the universe. Atheists would often argue that if God is truly good, then why would cruel and bad things happen all around us. To this, Lewis mentioned there was no easy answer (ibid, 39). He admitted that there are difficult questions that confront all of us, believers and non-believers alike. He also denounced the concept that Christianity should be made "simple" (ibid, 40). This is because simplicity often excludes many of the higher wisdoms of Christ, and would not explain many of the more difficult questions Christians may face. Lewis then went on to explore the many facets of dualism, that of the world having a polarized balance of a good power, and a bad power. In the Christian context, the bad power, which originally started out being wholesome and good, became corrupt. The bad power, otherwise known as Satan[45], is also believed to have been created by the good power, in this case God.

---

[43] Atheists are people who subscribe to atheism, which is the philosophy that denies the existence of any form of deity or deities. Atheism is also known as nontheism (Wikipedia, 2007).

[44] Pantheists are people who subscribe to the philosophical position of pantheism. Pantheism means "all god" in Greek, whereby it is believed that the entire universe is a single abstract "god", rather than a god being separate from the rest of the universe (Wikipedia, 2007).

[45] Satan, or "adversary" in Hebrew or "accuser" (Ha-Satan), is the fallen angel who stood against God, in Christianity. In Judaism, Satan is

From that, Lewis started to discuss the concept of free will. While God has the ultimate supernatural power to create just about anything, He had to give something extra to the higher beings He created – free will. Without free will, life and function will simply be a routine of automation, nothing else, nothing more. However, God so loved the humans He created, He gave them free will, the ability to choose, to decide on their own. With free will, humans can turn against God, but can also love and honor God, all on their own. Likewise, Satan, as an important angel before his fall from grace, was a powerful being with a will, and so, instead of loving and honoring God, he blasphemed and turned against God. Lewis then explained that sex was not what Satan taught to mankind, but rather, by tricking mankind to believe they would be "gods" themselves, that humans didn't need God. That was the greatest evil Satan did to both God and humankind (ibid, 49). However, Satan is doomed to fail, according to Lewis' assertions. This is because only God has the ability to provide eternal peace and happiness, and Satan or any other entity or thing, can never provide. Also, God gave something to humans that would allow humans to independently discern right and wrong – conscience. Therefore, while Satan can trick humans to turn away from God to seek peace and happiness, humankind will eventually realize there is no other way to find those except with embracing God.

In order to defeat Satan and his frequent onslaughts on mankind and God, God had to do something drastic. According to Lewis, God decided to land right into Satan's playground, as an entity called Jesus (ibid, 53). While Lewis mentioned that there are many theories to the life, death and resurrection of Christ, the main important thing for

---

supposed to be the accuser (or prosecutor), one of the divine council in Heaven (Wikipedia, Internet, 2007).

Christians to believe, and which make Christians true Christians, is that Christ died for us and his death washed our sins and gave us the potent formula to reach and unite with God again (ibid, 55). And because Christ was God and yet human, he combined both mortal human will (the ability to choose) and the Divine and infinite goodness, and so only His selfless sacrifice and death can truly redeem us.

Lewis then explained what it meant as a Christian process (ibid, 60), that of baptism, Holy Communion, the Mass, and the Lord's Supper. While denominations may differ in the mechanics of sacraments, it is important that Christians observe these processes, as they are pathways designed by God to lead to Him. While we live in imitation of Christ our Lord, it is important as Christians that we also know the concept of "Thine Will, not mine". Lewis also explained that when God comes back to this world, it would be too late for redemption. Therefore, while the human will is capable and willing, one must choose sides, and choose God (ibid, 65).

In Book 3 (ibid, 69), Lewis started by saying some people tend to associate moral perfection based on a set of rules and performance requirements as an ideal, which is something unachievable. Lewis then defined morality by associating it with three things (ibid, 72), fair play and harmony between people; harmonizing the innate qualities of people; and as something that affects the holistic human population at large. Lewis then illustrated that while many people tend to observe that of fair play and harmony between people, including that of erecting legislation and contract laws, much less is dedicated to enhancing the innate qualities of people or thinking and doing things for the greater universe, or that of being in communion with the ultimate entity, that of God.

Lewis then talked about two kinds of virtues (ibid, 76), Cardinal virtues, which he classified as virtues all civilized people recognize, and Theological virtues, which only Christians know about. Lewis explained that the Cardinal virtues are: prudence, temperance, justice, and fortitude.

Prudence can be defined as practical common sense (ibid, 77), where people contemplate on what they are doing at any one point in time, and also of its likely consequences. To contemplate, in Lewis' terms, requires intelligence and experience.

Temperance, according to Lewis, should not be equated with teetotalism, but that of moderation of all pleasures, rather than abstinence or to despise all pleasures and people who have pleasures (ibid, 78). Any insane or excessive attachment to any pleasure in particular, means a deviation from the Cardinal virtue of temperance.

Justice, according to Lewis, is not quite like how we may use it in contemporary terms of legislation and the judiciary, but that of fairness (ibid, 79). To Lewis, justice meant honesty, give and take, truthfulness, and keeping promises.

Fortitude was seen by Lewis as having the courage to face danger and pain (ibid, 79).

Lewis then further explained that having such Cardinal virtues does not simply mean exhibiting such actions infrequently, but rather, having such virtues so imbued and ingrained within a person that every action shows such Cardinal virtues in action. To Lewis, a person cannot simply do the right thing with no regard to how or why it was done (ibid, 80). Therefore, the means to the end is as important as the end itself, if in fact a person can be said to hold such Cardinal virtues. Lewis also mentioned that God does not want blind obedience, but rather, disciples who walk the talk and live a holy life in imitation of Christ. Lewis also further added that the sublime thinking behind a Christian must not be one of "as long as I adhere to these virtues this life", but one of continuity and permanence, showing that contemplative practice is in place to ingrain such Cardinal virtues within oneself throughout life.

Next, Lewis explained that Christian Scriptures do not give exact instructions to every minute detail, leaving to creative and innovative humans to figure out the details, as it should be (ibid, 83). For example, nowhere in the Bible was said that Christians must learn Hebrew or Greek, even thought the Bible gave instructions to learn and read the Bible. However, the New Testament did give plenty of hints how a fully Christian society might be like.

Lewis made comparisons of psychoanalysis[46], and Christian morality, and decided that psychoanalysis does not necessarily negate Christian thinking, but in fact, may overlap with parts of Christian morality. According to Lewis' assertion, when a person makes a moral choice it would involve an act of choosing, based on various feelings, impulses and prior conditioning as "raw materials" (ibid, 89). So in a classical case of a person having a bad psychological foundation which ultimately leads to a bad moral choice, Lewis reminded that it should not be seen as sin, which needs repentance, but rather, a disease, which requires healing. Also, while humans perceive only the superficial level of actions, Lewis asserted that God will judge based on moral choices, which can be hidden from public view. So an example of a wealthy person who gives lots of money away to charity and getting media coverage

---

[46] Psychoanalysis is a cluster of theories and methods started by psychologist Sigmund Freud. It is used as part of psychotherapy, to discern unconscious parts of a person's mental processes, so as to find particular counseling or treatment for the person (Wikipedia, 2007).

(typically with tax benefits hidden from public view), may count less in God's eyes than an anonymous person who rescues a small animal despite having a medical phobia of animals and an allergy from animal fur.

Lewis also illustrated that Christian morality is not bargaining chips for Christians to put on good behavior in exchange for "favors" from God (ibid, 92). Rather, Lewis believes it is part of a contemplative practice for a Christian to become a better, more righteous, and more attuned disciple of Christ, whenever such morality is repeated over and over again.

Next, Lewis explored the issue of sexual propriety (ibid, 94), one of the most unpopular Christian virtues in Lewis' assertion, which covers the range of decency, modesty, and chastity. Christianity is different from many other religions in that intimacy within the confines of a legitimate marriage, is not necessarily despised (unlike some other faiths which views the act itself as vile). At the same time, the animal instinct within ordinary human beings rises above reason and virtue, and is not easily subdued or transformed. Lewis added that while lust is certainly not good, having a hating, evil heart is a lot worse:

"... A cold, self-righteous prig who goes regularly to church may be far nearer to hell than a prostitute. But, of course, it is better to be neither."

From desires, a Christian should obey the law and abide in a rightful marriage, since Christ said that a man and wife are to be regarded as a single organism ("one flesh") (ibid, 104). Therefore, sexual union between a married couple cannot be divorced into the sexual act and the rest of the mental and emotional union. Therefore, in the Christian context, a marriage must be for life and divorce is not a concept within the theology (ibid, 105). At the same time, a marriage must conform to another virtue, that of justice or keeping a promise. In ancient times, a promise is absolutely binding in word, without the possibility of unbinding it without sacrificing honor. Of course, in the contemporary world, many people might have forgotten the sanctity of promises, and the worldly contract laws came into the picture to prevent people from negating promises supposedly made solemnly.

Another difficult concept is that a Christian wife has to obey her husband (ibid, 112), especially in the contemporary context of sexual equality and opportunity. Many modern women have become very successful in every field traditionally held by men, while still being able to juggle their careers with the taking care of children and the home. Lewis made an honest admission that he was not married and so his views in this area may be contested. But Lewis made an interesting and reasonable conclusion, that in Christianity, a man is seen as the "head" of the family, because all external relations and disputes, if any, have to be managed and resolved by the men. Lewis' assertion is that women have a natural maternal tendency to protect the family, and therefore would be more likely unfair to outsiders, than would men. So in difficult and alarming situations that involve outsiders, it would make more sense, to Lewis, that the men take on the leadership or diplomatic position (ibid, 114).

Lewis then proceeded to contradict his earlier assertion that chastity is the most unpopular of Christian virtues, by saying that perhaps forgiveness is even more unpopular and difficult (ibid, 115). Especially in the context of the Second World War when Lewis was speaking to British soldiers, it would seem impossible for the British to forgive the Germans under the rule of Hitler, and the atrocities some of the Germans have done against the Jews. In a typical example often seen on local television, the immediate family of someone who died in a tragic car accident would scream on live television they will never forgive the person who caused their relative's death. However, in Christianity, it is important that although we can hate the sin, we must not hate the sinner, and that is one of the most important things to remember as a pastor or chaplain, lest we lapse into arrogance and bigotry.

Another difficult concept is "thou shalt not kill", which seem to imply any warfare or killing is bad. However, in ancient Hebrew, as quoted in Matthew, Mark and Luke, Christ quoted the commandment with the Greek equivalent of "murder", rather than "kill". Therefore, there is a distinction between murder and killing, as Lewis explained, as not all killing is murder (while all murder is killing) similar to not all sexual activity is adultery. He defended the historical incidents of Christian knights who fought for a good cause, versus pacifists who insisted that all killing is bad (ibid, 119). Lewis further expounded that while killing may be necessary in some rare circumstances, one must not hate, or enjoy hating others. The rising of hate within oneself is the mark of the fallen Christian (ibid, 120).

The great sin as Lewis called it, is pride or self-conceit (ibid, 121), while the opposite is humility, one of the hallmark virtues of Christian morals. Lewis used the example of the devil Satan, whose pride prompted him to turn against God, and subsequently fell from grace. Therefore, if even great angels can fall from grace just because of pride, then humility must be the master-key to unlock a Christ-filled life. Lewis even used the comparison of greed against pride, and concluded that greed can only drive a person to go so far while pride can drive a person much deeper into the abyss (ibid, 123). Even for God-fearing Christians, the devil often tempts through pride by attempting to reinforce the concept that humans can be good and valuable, that Christians can fall from a closeness with God. Lewis asserted that the worst form of pride is when someone looks down on others so much that the person does not even care what others think of him/her. Lewis also added a warning that when a person thinks he is not conceited, then he might just be very conceited (ibid, 128).

Lewis then presented the three Theological virtues, of faith, hope, and charity (ibid, 129).

Lewis expanded on the concept of charity, where forgiveness is a facet of charity, but also that of love. However, Lewis explained that the "love" in Christian charity is not an emotion but the human will that expresses actions to others. Charity is not patronizing, and it rises above sentimentality or pity.

Lewis then talked about the Theological virtue of hope (ibid, 134). Lewis challenged the readers to not just focus on microscopic issues, but rather, to expand on much bigger things, as a foundation of having hope as a Christian virtue. Lewis explained there are three paths of dealing with hope, the "fool's" way, the "disillusioned" way, and the "Christian" way (ibid, 136). The "fool's" way is a feeble attempt to find the next best (or better) thing, in the hope that things might turn out better. The "disillusioned" way seems to confront many older persons, where they have experienced a great many events in life, and possibly faced many disappointments, and attempts to justify failure and sadness with reason. The Christian way, is to focus on finding God, and see that everything we experience can be a sign to lead us closer to God. That is true hope in the Christian context.

Lewis explored the third Theological virtue of faith (ibid, 138), which is often the centerpiece of Christian belief, and often the source of argument with non-Christians. Lewis calls the Christian virtue of faith as one where you hold on to certain beliefs that at one time, your reason had accepted, despite one's changing moods (ibid, 140). Lewis cautioned that Christians must not imagine Christian faith to be either an examination, or a bargain with God. God is eternal and does not partake in such trivia. But Lewis challenged readers to rise to a higher level of faith, that of trusting God, rather than simply accepting intellectually theories about God.

In Book 4 (ibid, 153), Lewis started on the basics of Christian theology. While some people may not feel the need for theology especially if they have truly experienced the grace of God, Lewis explained that theology is like a map, without which one cannot navigate very well, that is, theology has a real practical purpose rather than simply being academic (contrary to some people's beliefs). Lewis used the analogy of a statue to show that even though a statue may look like a man, it is not alive. Likewise, while man takes on the likeness of God, man is not God. Therefore, only through Christ our Redeemer can we once again unite with God (ibid, 158, 181).

Lewis then attempted to explain the concept of the Triune God, that of the Father, the Son, and the Holy Spirit, by equating that with the principles of dimensional physics (ibid, 162, 172). So God has a pervasive form to most of us, that of the Father. But God also took on a human form, in a recognizable form to us, as Jesus Christ. There is also another "dimension" to God, that of the Holy Spirit, which rather than one looking at the Spirit, the Spirit acts through a believer instead (ibid, 176).

Lewis then attempted to illustrate the pervasiveness of the power and majesty of God, where God can do anything, at anywhere, and yet attend to billions of people all at the same time (ibid, 167). Lewis extrapolated that God must not be operating in a linear fashion such as how we go through life in a linear fashion. God cannot be bound by the confines of time as we know it. God is not bound by a past, present, and future.

On a cautionary note, Lewis also explained that God does not want "toy soldiers" of His people (ibid, 183), but rather, sons. Therefore, God gave humans free will, rather than simply create automatons or "toy soldiers" to simply do His bidding. And Lewis explained further that by calling "Father", humans are in fact acknowledging God as Father, and also inferring humans are sons. But by acknowledging God as Father, humans must also recognize that it cannot be frivolous, since the relationship between Father and sons, must be one of imitation of Christ (since Jesus Christ is the Son of God). And by imitation, Lewis warned that it should not be a façade or pretense, but rather, one of "mirroring" the qualities and virtues of Christ (ibid, 190).

Lewis next explored the seemingly paradoxical path of Christianity, in that the path can seem easy, or very difficult (ibid, 195). On the one hand, by trusting and having faith, God will provide, nurture, protect, and enlighten, which makes the path "easy". On the other hand, Christian virtues are binding values that must be steadfastly observed, not just talked about, which can be a lifelong struggle since humans will constantly falter and fall, making the path "difficult". However, Lewis asserted that the bottomline is, Christians must lean on Christ, which will increasingly empower Christians to lead a proper, Christ-filled righteous life, and the path will become increasingly clearer, brighter, "easier". By leaning to God, Christians will allow God to make them whole and perfect (ibid, 202), and will always pull humans from the rubble and dust when they fall (ibid, 203). When the author received ordination from his Lutheran archbishop, the archbishop's reminders were, "my brother, know that the path ahead will be painful and difficult". Therefore, likewise, Lewis mentioned that if we let God,

God will make us perfect, even as the path is necessarily difficult, challenging, and painful (ibid, 205).

When we talk of God's irresistible grace, we know that for many human failings, there are still nice people around. However, Lewis asserted that the niceness of people is not something that springs forth independently from humans, but bestowed by the grace of God (ibid, 214). Likewise, power and wealth are also assets bestowed by God, intended that individuals blessed by such power and wealth, to do God's bidding to help others, and not for frivolous gains or self-glorification (ibid, 215).

Lewis closed his talks with explanation of what "born-again" Christians meant. For Christians, accepting Christ and thereafter receiving baptism, and then walking the path and in imitation of Christ, made such people "new men" (ibid, 218). To be truly "new men" and to continue the path closer and closer to God, Lewis reminded that Christians must give up their selves, or ego, so that God can bestow a "new personality" to the Christians. Simply talking and articulating about Christianity does not make a true Christian. Rather, a believer must completely let go of his own ego and self, and in so doing, allowing Christ to empower the believer to find the true self.

Top 5 Themes and Why

Lewis' book made an enjoyable read, especially for questioning skeptics who love debate, as well as new Christians in search of truth in an easy-to-read manner.

Lewis spent a considerable amount of time to articulate the law of human nature, which differs from many of the natural laws of physics. This is important as it showed that human nature is very complex, and in providing pastoral care, one must be aware of the constant transient nature of how humans react, and be ready to challenge and yet comfort Christians.

Another important theme is the difference between Pantheism and Christianity. This can be very important in segregating orthodoxy from other paths.

Lewis' explanation of Cardinal and Theological virtues are also another important theme, making it very clear in human terms, without dwelling on deeper theological references. This can be important for new Christians to assimilate.

Lewis' use of "toy soldiers" as a metaphor for automatons was vivid and imaginative, and very useful in allowing ministers to use that as a reference of God's gift of free will to mankind.

Lastly, Lewis reminded that even as Christianity seems easy, God does have demands of us. The important thing for Christians is to continuously lean on God for nourishment and nurture, and to walk in imitation of Christ our Redeemer.

Author's Notes

Lewis used very vivid and imaginative themes and metaphors, to help explain Christianity in a palatable manner, especially to skeptics or new believers.

Therefore, this book serves an important purpose for ministering to skeptics in this side of the world where cultural sensitivity and gentility are admired and sometimes demanded. By using imaginative themes and stories, a minister can help bridge the gap between total disbelief from people, and the high theology that Christian academics and clergy are used to. The author found that a good storyteller like Lewis can do a lot more for people, especially in a situation of duress (such as war, in the context of Lewis' book). Therefore, as the author moves forward, he will be reminded that in difficult situations, it will help to sometimes explore more creative means to explain Christianity to others.

Christian Theology Primer

Christian Theology Primer

Abstract

One of the forefathers of systematic Protestant theology was John Calvin, who wrote the "Institutes of the Christian Religion"[47] in 1536.

Many centuries later, Erickson's "Christian Theology" provides a contemporary context into systematic theology, meant as a study book for Christians of any vocation, whether lay or clergy. His work, revised in 2006, attempted to address growing Christian populations outside the "traditional" locations such as Americas, Europe, and Central Asia, so that the work can be relevant to the diversity of ethnic and cultural differences worldwide, including that of Asia Pacific. In Asia Pacific, Christianity is certainly growing organically, whereby evangelism is slowly taking root, even in countries where the resident faiths are very entrenched. Erickson's work can therefore provide a practical and theoretical framework for practicing ministers and missionaries, as well as would-be ministers and missionaries.

The book goes through the process of knowing the emergence of God as we know Him, in His history, actions, and revelations. The book also provides a framework for what humanity means, and how humanity relates to sin, the Redeemer in Christ, the Holy Spirit, and how humanity can receive salvation. Then Erickson

---

[47] John Calvin (1509-1564 AD) was a French Protestant thinker during the Reformation and he developed Calvinism, which were closely related to Martin Luther's reformation theology. He wrote "Institutes of the Christian Religion" (or Christianae Religions Institutio in Latin) in 1536. The work was an attempt by Calvin and many other theologians, to develop a method or system of religious study that combined sacred texts, history, philosophy, science and ethics (Wikipedia, 2007).

addressed the concept of the universal church, as well as eschatology[48].

In Part 1 (Erickson, 2006, 17), Erickson discussed the concept of theology, that of studying God. Erickson started by explaining that while humans can attempt to structure sciences, present arts, and perform physical feats, religion remains one of the ultimate frontiers that sometimes defy explanation, or is open to schism and diversity, without any possible unity in plain sight.

Erickson explained that one of the hallmarks of religion, rather than science per se, is that of the expression of personal experience (ibid, 21). For example, often in our churches, pastors would call on the congregation to share witnessing events, whereby personal events, incidents, healings, and other spiritually inspired experiences, are shared and discussed. Religion must be built on an endless loop of faith, study, contemplation, and action steps. Therefore, Christians sharing spiritually charged and inspired incidents with others, is an expression of the practice of religion.

Erickson gave a succinct definition of theology, which he described as the "study or science of God" (ibid, 22). According to Erickson, theology must be biblical, systematic, conforming to general culture and learning, contemporary, and most of all, practical (ibid, 24).

Erickson also dispelled the notion that simply loving Christ does not make a true Christian. The study and contemplation of the doctrine and scripture are equally important (ibid, 29). Therefore, theology has a strong place

---

[48] Eschatology is the study of the end-times, where the end of the world and the final destiny of humanity are extrapolated, discussed and taught (Wikipedia, 2007).

in any Christian's lifelong journey of sanctification and communion with God.

While Erickson explained the various forms of secular philosophy, a quote from Martin Luther perhaps summed up what could be seen as the great divide between secular philosophy and theology, "Let philosophy remain within her bounds, as God has appointed, and let us make sure of her as a character in a comedy" (ibid, 41).

Erickson discussed the various forms of studying theology, and concluded that as time goes by, a systematic theologian would find it difficult to cover the entire spectrum of doctrines (ibid, 66). In the perspective of the author, he would humbly believe that Erickson's view is agreeable, especially since the spectrum of God's kingdom is vast and beyond human reasoning, and it is perhaps agreeable to only focus on areas of systematic theology that can be grasped within mortal means, rather than to stray wide and far but lacking depth altogether.

Erickson outlined the process of studying theology (ibid, 70), which would include the collection of biblical materials, the summarizing of the collected materials, an analysis on the collected materials, a comparison to historical evidence, a consultation with various cultural perspectives to put the theology in a real-world context, the distillation of the doctrine into digestible forms, adding supporting evidence from non-biblical sources, putting into a contemporary context all that has been collated and distilled, developing a central theme, and finally, creating a structured framework and system for others to study beyond the central theme.

The Bible is not without its critics, even today. However, it can be said that many critics, when criticizing the Bible, may not have studied in depth like a typical theologian, but rely heavily on flawed arguments. Erickson dedicated a chapter (ibid, 85) to the various forms of criticism of the Bible (Old and New Testament alike), to show that while criticism itself can be negative, it is also important for apologetics, evangelists, missionaries and disciples, to be able to defend Christianity by understanding the various forms and methods employed by critics. For example, one of the classical flawed methods of criticism is the use of circular reasoning[49].

Next, Erickson talked about making the Christian message current and relevant to the modern, changing world (ibid, 115). Erickson mentioned Rudolf Bultmann[50] who tried to erase the portions of the Bible that to Bultmann, were mythology. Bultmann thought that by removing the miraculous portions of the Bible, including that of the resurrection of Christ (which is central to the Apostle's Creed[51]), the remaining would be more "appealing" to the skeptics, and may therefore help to convert them to Christianity. However, Bultmann's views were not accepted by the mainstream orthodox Christians, and remained a curious philosopher divided and ostracized

---

[49] Circular reasoning, a fallacy in argument, sometimes employed during litigation or debates, is best illustrated by an example. In the case of a lawyer attempting to use circular reasoning on an innocent victim accused of defaming someone, he may say, "the defendant has shown no remorse," which thereby imply that IF the defendant is guilty, being one with no remorse, means that the defendant is an evil person, and by inference, must be guilty (Wikipedia, 2007).

[50] Rudolf Karl Bultmann (1884-1976 AD) was a Lutheran theologian, but one who controversially tried to remove all portions of the Bible that talked about miracles and signs, and relied on excessive criticism of the Bible to try to appeal to more contemporary or skeptical people (Wikipedia, 2007).

[51] The Apostle's Creed (or Symbolum Apostolorum in Latin) is often read and affirmed during Holy Communion at Reformed churches as well as many orthodox and Catholic churches. One of the central beliefs is the resurrection of Christ after being crucified to death on a cross (Wikipedia, 2007).

from many Christian theologians. Erickson mentioned two approaches of making theology modern, including the "Transformers" (ibid, 123) who attempt to change the Bible altogether, discarding parts of the Bible deemed too ancient or impractical in modern times; and the "Translators" (ibid, 126) who attempt to paraphrase parts of the Bible, hoping to retrofit or force-fit the ancient text into modern contexts. The danger of both these approaches is deviating from orthodoxy. Also, many of these liberals do not see the reality of personal witnessing experiences, and dismiss them as either irrelevant or unreal altogether. They do not believe in the mysteries of faith that which has strengthened Christianity and the believers' faith through the ages.

Erickson next discussed the issue of religious language (ibid, 135) and the reactions such language invokes in believers, and skeptics. Skeptics often dismiss religious language as meaningless, while believers often map religious language to their sensory, and sometimes extra-sensory experiences, and perceive that the Bible is inerrant, and its language reasonable.

Erickson then discussed pre-modernism, modernism, and post-modernism (ibid, 158). Pre-modernism expounds on the rationality of the formation of the universe and its state, but with a supernatural element and a purpose to the existence of this universe. Modernism agrees with some of pre-modernism, except that it does not believe there is a supernatural element to the formation of the universe nor its ongoing existence. Therefore, modernism does not believe there is any God, and that humans are the reason to the ongoing existence of the world, at least where the humans are staying. The problem with modernism is manyfold, one of which is the lack of rational explanation of the presence of ethics and conscience in humans (ibid, 165), which is not present in all other animals. That is such an esoteric design that modernists find no way to explain it.

Post-modernism takes several forms, one of which is conservative or restorative post-modernism (ibid, 168), which Erickson mentioned Pope John Paul II as an example. Conservative post-modernists resemble pre-modernists except that they accept modern discoveries and insights.

In Part 2 (ibid, 177), Erickson discussed how God manifests Himself to humans, through revelations. Humans are often doubting and finite, and therefore, for an infinite God to communicate with very finite and limited humans, God must manifest through some kind of signs, or revelations. There are two kinds of revelations – general revelations, and special revelations. General revelations are demonstrated through nature, history, and the inner being of humans themselves. Humans are somewhat alike in physiology and anatomy with other animals, but yet they are decidedly different in the sense that they walk continuously upright, and are capable of directed free will and moral judgment. Erickson went into the analysis of the passages in the Bible and how various theologians interpreted the passages, including Karl Barth[52], Martin Luther, John Calvin, and so on. However, many of the theologians, such as Barth, did not put forth entirely convincing arguments, since much of the Christian faith depends also on God's special revelations (ibid, 200), which are to be innately experienced by believing Christians, and therefore are hard to prove or disprove. At the same time, because of the original sin and the ongoing sins of humans, given to failing as consistently as God is flawless, therefore, God's special revelations become even more important in today's context. When we describe God as Father, there is already an acknowledgement of a personal and emotive relationship

---

[52] Karl Barth (1886-1968 AD) was a Swiss reformed theologian, who was considered one of the pioneers of the Neo-Orthodox movement, who tried to bring Christian back to the Orthodox ways and to free theology from the liberals (Wikipedia, 2007).

with God. Although there is utmost respect and reverence and sometimes respectful fear, there is also a relational love between God and us. Therefore, God's special revelations are often revealed in intimately personal experiences throughout history right up to contemporary times, and are aimed to strengthen our faith and conviction.

One of the hallmarks of the Bible is that it is inspiring (ibid, 226). While the Bible tells of historical instances, analogies and parables in rather poetic ways, as well as having terrifying stories of punitive measures against sin, the underlying message is often one that urges us on with inspiration, and empowers us to be able to stride forward with greater confidence and strength. Inspiration in the Bible takes two paths, one of supernatural occurrences, and one of ordinary but entirely moving emotive events.

Erickson discussed one of the most contested arenas whenever the Bible is discussed – its inerrancy (ibid, 246). Liberal Christians, heretics and non-believers would often doubt or deem dubious, portions, passages, or even the entire book of the Bible. Orthodox apologetic Christians would be polarized to the other end of the spectrum, in the absolute inerrancy of the Bible. The inerrancy of the Bible is not a frivolous debate for philosophical reasons, but one that makes Christianity dependable for believers from ancient times to the end times. If the inerrancy of the Bible is doubted, faith would diminish, churches would fall, and humans would stray farther away from God in an already turbulent world. In some subtle and distinct areas of the Bible, such as that of Genesis, there is still ongoing debate amongst steadfast Christian theologians about various dates and emergences of the events. But science often consistently fails at some point, where rational and scientific explanation cannot fully explain parts of the Bible, nor can science disprove the Bible. Therefore, it might be wise for humans to simply admit, without arrogance, that God does transcend our frequent and earnest attempts to reach full understanding, and that the Bible can be relied upon (ibid, 270). John Calvin described that "humans in the natural state are unable to recognize and respond to divine truth" (ibid, 282), which allowed us to comprehend our limited intellectual capacity to grasp the infinite nature of God and His infinite wisdom expressed through the Bible.

In Part 3 (ibid, 289), Erickson described his understanding of what God is like. Erickson showed that God exhibited several attributes, of spirituality, personality, life, infinity, and constancy. God is in spirit form (ibid, 294), in that He is not made of mundane matter that He has created. God also has a personality, including names, being personal with believers, has individuality, self-consciousness, will, and feelings (ibid, 295). God has life, affirmed by His words "I am" (rather than in the past tense), showing that He is a living God (ibid, 297). God is infinite (ibid, 298), and Erickson described as God as unlimitable, rather than unlimited. Therefore, God is also omni-present and can transcend space. God transcends time in that He has always been. God's knowledge and wisdom is also infinite, whereby He knows all things, and is infinitely wise. God is infinite also in terms of His emotions. God shows constancy (ibid, 304), whereby we can always depend on Him. His divine nature has always been, and will always be.

While we often marvel at God's majesty, we must also remember God is infinitely good (ibid, 309). God is holy, righteous, just, genuine, truthful, faithful, compassionate, persistent, and shows infinite grace. One of the special qualities of God is His grace, which exhibits in ways beyond many other faiths.

God is both immanent and transcendent (ibid, 327), whereby the Bible said that God is active and present in His creation and the universe, but also far beyond and superior to anything He has created. For many Christians, only Sundays seem to be dedicated to God, while in fact, every breath one takes should be a constant reminder of God's transcendence and immanence in life and throughout creation.

One of the interesting interpretations about God's immanence and transcendence was by Paul Tillich[53] (ibid, 333), which is still disputed by many theologians. Tillich believed that God is not a being as we imagine, but more like some kind of internal power or force that causes everything to exist. In Tillich's argument, only finite beings exist. Since God is infinite, God cannot simply exist, but just is. But Tillich's argument also led to the cessation of prayer, one of the hallmarks of being Christian, and so is not recommended as prayer is central to the belief system of Christians, besides study and contemplation.

The triune God (ibid, 346) is a unique feature and theological foundation of Christianity, one that seems to be absent from all other faiths in the world. Even those faiths such as Orthodox Judaism and Islam, which share many similar elements, do not believe in the triune God of the Father, the Son Jesus Christ, and the Holy Spirit. Although Orthodox Judaism denies the existence of the triune God, the Bible, especially the Old Testament (which forms the foundational scriptures of Judaism), does speak of God in plural forms. For example, sometimes God was addressed as "elohim", which is a plural God. Also, in Genesis 1:26 (ibid, 354), God said, "Let us make man in our image". However, although God manifests as the Father, the Son, and the Holy Spirit, there are not three gods, but one God.

---

[53] Paul Johannes Tillich (1886-1965 AD) was a German-American Protestant theologian and apologist, seen by many mainstream theologians as an atheist (Wikipedia, 2007).

In Part 4 (ibid, 371), Erickson further discussed the different suppositions of whether God's plan is predestined (or foreordained) compared to human-created plans (ibid, 375). The Calvinists[54] believe in predestination or foreordination of events, whereby God has a pre-existing plan that takes place. Arminians[55] believe otherwise, in that the human free will prevails and therefore plans fall into place. However, Erickson suggested that a mildly Calvinistic model might address the issue of God's plan versus human plans might work better, whereby God's intended plan is congruent with the free will of humans, thereby meeting or merging together into a common plan of action (ibid, 385).

Creation (ibid, 391), as described in the book of Genesis, must surely be the most debated part of the Bible, in that even among Christian denominations, there is much dispute. However, the Apostle's Creed clearly stated, "I believe in God the Father Almighty, Maker of heaven and earth" (ibid, 393), and the Creed is affirmed by most mainstream Christians sharing communion. One of the hallmarks of God's creation is that it is beyond description, scientific understanding, and completely creative. Very few can dispute the creative genius of the world and the universe we exist in, and to simply think it is a random freak event is to deride such an awesome creation.

---

[54] Calvinist theology stressed on the total depravity of humans, unconditional election of certain persons to salvation, limited atonement of Christ (only for the elect), irresistible Grace (versus the human will), and the perseverance of the Saints.

[55] Arminian theology stressed on election based on foreknowledge, unlimited atonement for all people, the inability of humans to save themselves and need the Holy Spirit to cleanse and create a "new birth", prevenient Grace of the Holy Spirit to allow humans to yearn to learn the gospel and lean to God for salvation, and conditional perseverance of believers (whereby people have to continuously seek the Grace of God and walk in the light, rather than turn from Grace).

God does not simply create and leave His creation alone. His providence (ibid, 412) is demonstrated in the continuing grace He extends and manifests throughout creation and throughout time even today. God also demonstrates His special possible treatments of sin. God can prevent sin, but He does not always prevent sin. God can steer sin in more positive outcomes, and He can limit the outcome of sin. God also shows His special providence to those who engage in prayer (ibid, 430). God wants human believers to be relational with Him, and prayer is an active mechanism for humans to bridge God's providence.

On the topic of evil (ibid, 436), Erickson asked several questions, that of why evil continue to exist throughout time, even as God is omnipotent and compassionate. There are two kinds of evils, that of natural evil in the form of destructive forces of nature such as earthquakes, hurricanes, storms and volcano eruptions. There is also moral evil, which is driven by humans themselves, against other humans. On sin, Erickson explained that God certainly did not create sin, but merely provided the means and options available for human free will. Therefore, only humans and the fallen angels have sinned, not God (ibid, 454). At the same time, we must not think that suffering or calamity we experience is a direct translation or manifestation of some specific sin. For example, if we are born blind, it does not necessarily imply we committed a particular sin to be born blind (ibid, 454). God in fact, is deeply grieved by humans sinning against Him, as said in Genesis 6:6, much as a loving father would be deeply grieved when a child turns into a criminal and is ultimately jailed for his crimes. On the issue of hell, it is the same as a human's choice of turning to sin. Some people would consistently turn God away throughout life, telling God to "go away" or "leave me alone". Therefore, due to the cumulative mental state of such people, ultimately God grants the wishes of such people, which is the state of hell itself.

The concept of angels and demons (ibid, 457) form a great deal of Christian and other belief systems. Angels are superhuman with special powers and abilities, but are limited when compared to God. Most people are not able to see angels in physical form, unless allowed by God to see. Angels are God's messengers and they glorify and praise God. At the same time, angels minister to believers, and protect them from harm. Against enemies, angels execute judgment. And in the second coming, angels will accompany God. Demons are fallen angels who were banished by God when they lost their holiness, affinity and obedience to God. Some of the tricks of demons include deception and temptation, which they use against humans.

In Part 5 (ibid, 479), Erickson discussed the doctrine of humanity, since humans are the highest creatures God created on earth, in His image and likeness, and that He has blessed humans with free will in order to seek love and communion with Him.

One interesting story was told of God's "time", when it comes to creation (ibid, 501). A king wanted to see works of God. A counselor told the king to plant four acorns. When the king planted them, he saw four fully-grown trees. He thought a miracle had occurred. However, his counselor told him eighty years had passed, and then the king realized that he has aged a great deal. The king became angry and proclaimed there was no miracle after all. However, his counselor reminded him that it was still God's work in action, whether it was one second, or eighty years. The story was told as a reminder that God's work exists in all places at all time, and does not require immediacy, unlike how some fundamentalists seem to demand (ibid, 501).

Humans are finite and transient in their existence, knowledge, wisdom, and performance of actions. This contrasts greatly with God, who is infinite. However, Christians must not beat down their own actions since every highest actions of mankind can be as high as humanly possible, actions to glorify God.

Both Martin Luther and John Calvin believe that humans only retain fragments (ibid, 523) of the likeness to God, much like relics or remnants, since humans are corrupted by original sin and ongoing sins. However, God still intends the uncorrupted image for humans, even though such a pristine condition and image is not present in us. The only "person" who could demonstrate such a pristine and uncorrupted condition was Jesus Christ.

Humans show three elements, according to the trichotomism hypothesis commonly propositioned by conservative Protestants (ibid, 538). According to the hypothesis, humans have a material body, a psychological body or "soul", and a spirit, which resonates with spirituality. It is the presence of the three elements that make humans different from other animals and plants. An alternative is dichotomism, which describes humans as having a material body and a soul or spirit (ibid, 540). Yet another alternative is monism, which describes humans has a singular inseparable being since a human must be defined by a material body and to think a spirit roaming without a material body is unthinkable (ibid, 543). However, Erickman explained that a more probable way to explain human nature is conditional unity (ibid, 557), where humans are seen as unities, being complex and whose nature cannot be easily reduced to elements.

When God created humankind, He made no distinction to ethnicity, gender, or economic status (ibid, 558). The diversity was embraced by God as all of His creation, and the prejudices are all humans' own creation. Erickson dispelled the myths and arrogant falsehoods of some people who prejudiced against certain races, as well as the female gender (ibid, 564). Also, one must not neglect or disrespect the aged, for God's Bible also valued the aged (ibid, 568). For example, ancient Hebrews and the Orientals (the Chinese) held the aged in utmost respect, as the aged demonstrated learned wisdom and deep experience in life (ibid, 569). God also does not prejudice against the unborn child, or an unmarried person (whether male or female).

In Part 6 (ibid, 579), Erickson discussed the concept of sin, in relation to Christian theology. The causes of sin include ignorance (especially willful ignorance), error, and inattention (ibid, 585). The characteristics of sin is more varied, including simply missing the mark (implying falling short of God's commands rather than willful disregard), impiety, transgression, iniquity (lacking in integrity), obvious rebellion (against God's Word), treachery (betrayal of God), perversion, and abomination (causing not just objection, but revulsion in God).

James 1:13 mentioned, "When tempted, no one should say, 'God is tempting.' For God cannot be tempted by evil, nor does He tempt anyone." Therefore, Erickson stressed that it is very important to note that sin is not caused by God (ibid, 613). All sin stems from human desires. Erickson claimed that some desires are legitimate, although it might be clear to note that all desires, which can grow over time, will corrupt and ultimately, cause problems for all humans. Conversely, asceticism and abstinence (from any desire) is not correct either, unless the spirit and soul of the person is already free from these to begin with. Erickson mentioned that perhaps the way to free oneself from sin is through education (ibid, 617).

Why is sin bad? The problem with sin is that it not only corrupts the human soul and spirit, it has painful side effects (ibid, 618). One side effect is the falling out of favor with our God, which perhaps is the most disastrous side effect of all. Other side effects include guilt, punishment (legally, psychologically or spiritually), and death. Death can come in the form of physical death (ibid, 629), if a commonly acknowledged heinous crime demands capital punishment by death. Death can also mean spiritual death (ibid, 631), which is impairment in that a solid barrier stands between sinners and God. Death also comes in the form of eternal death (ibid, 631), which implies that at the time of physical death, should the sinner also has spiritual death (which means no communion with God), then a permanent eternal death results. Sin will cause a sinner to experience enslavement, detachment from reality, denial, self-deception, insensitivity, self-centeredness, restlessness, aggressive competitiveness, lack of empathy, rejection of authority, and the inability to love (ibid, 632).

Erickson discussed original sin (ibid, 637), and concluded that we inherited from the first man Adam, his sin, the resultant corrupted nature, a sense of guilt, and the condemnation that comes with it. Unless we believe and are baptized, we will not have any salvation.

In Asia alone, there is an increasing unveiling of corporate and non-profit failings, and more and more people are beginning to doubt and inspect the operations of corporations and non-profits. In the same light, while Christians have traditionally been aware of personal sins, there is a need to become more aware of social sins that operate in the context of our world (ibid, 657). While the world is inherently doomed by prior judgment and is awaiting a future execution of that judgment, faithful believers of Christ will not need to be afraid (ibid, 663).

In Part 7 (ibid, 677), Erickson then discussed the person of Christ, the person central to the belief of any Christian, whether Orthodox, Catholic, or Protestant. Without an understanding of Jesus Christ the person, one cannot truly claim to be a Christian. There seems more and more interest to probe into the historical Jesus Christ, with the emergence of many blockbuster movies that talked about relics and events that surrounded the life of Christ. However, while skeptics would try to demolish the reality of Christ despite many witnessing experiences and especially doubting the inerrancy of the Bible, Christians must be steadfast to know that Christ is exactly how the Bible portrayed Him to be as deity (ibid, 700), especially when the Bible itself stood the test of time and scrutiny, such as "But I say to all of you: In the future you will see the Son of Man sitting at the right hand of the Mighty One and coming on the clouds of heaven." (Matthew 26: 63) Why is the deity of Christ important? The deity of Christ implies that we can gain real knowledge of God, since Jesus taught us many things about God. The deity of Christ also brings real redemption, as He sacrificed His life for us. The deity of Christ also brings communion once again, between God and man, exalted through prayer (ibid, 720). But at the same time, the humanity of Christ (ibid, 721) must not be diminished or negated, even as the concept of Christ as a human being is not as hotly debated as the deity of Christ. And though Christ was definitely human, He differed from us with His holiness and sinless nature (ibid, 735), and therefore, as a human being united with God (ibid, 749), He could redeem us by offering Himself as the ultimate sacrifice.

And though Jesus was man, He was also having God in Him. Therefore, His birth was one of a miraculous nature, sometimes called "virgin birth" and sometimes called "virgin conception" (ibid, 756). Though theologians still argue about how the conception happened and the process itself, the bottom-line was that Jesus was not conceived through any sexual intercourse, but simply passed through Virgin Mary and was born in a miraculous way, so that He would be both human and divine. And as God's greatest gift of grace (ibid, 774), God showed the world that He continued to care for His sons, by bringing a special gift in the form of Jesus, to the world. Jesus Christ's virgin conception can best be seen as one of the mysteries of our faith.

In Part 8 (ibid, 779), Erickson discussed the works of Christ, and how those works influenced our beliefs. Christ has three functions, that of bringing God's revelations to us, ruling over the world through His church on earth even today, and acting in an intercessory role on behalf of us sinners to our Father in Heaven (ibid, 787). And Christ works through two stages, which continues today. First, he went through the stage of humiliation (ibid, 788), whereby He came to our world as a human, died ignobly, and descended into hell on our behalf. Then Christ went through the second stage of exaltation (ibid, 794), with His rising from the dead, ascending into Heaven and sitting at the right hand side of God, and eventually, the Second Coming in full glory.

Christ died for us for a good reason, to atone for our sins, and to afford redemption to us from God (ibid, 798). How He did it was through an ancient belief of sacrifice, by offering Himself as the ultimate sacrifice being a sinless and pure person, to appease God's anger against sin, even as God loves His creations. John the Baptist said, "Look, the Lamb of God, who takes away the sin of the world!" (John 1:29) Christ also provided Himself as a substitute sacrifice for us (ibid, 830), where He died on our behalf, and in doing so, reconciled us with God once again. While Calvinists would comment that Christ's atonement is partial, in that this atonement only redeems the elected few, other theologians would point to God's universal grace, and that Christ's atonement was for all, as said above in John 1:29. However, it is Erickson's view, that though atonement is made available for all (ibid, 852), only the believers and the baptized can truly receive this divine gift.

In Part 9 (ibid, 861), Erickson discussed the much-needed knowledge of the Holy Spirit. In 1 Corinthians 3:16-17, Paul said, "Don't you know that you yourselves are God's temple and that Gods Spirit lives in you? If anyone destroys God's temple, God will destroy him; for God's temple is sacred, and you are that temple" (ibid, 874). Therefore, in Erickson's explanation, Paul's assertion was that God and the Holy Spirit was interchangeable, thereby putting to rest some minority's misaligned thinking that Holy Spirit is "lesser" than God. With Paul's sayings, it is clear that the Father, the Son Jesus Christ, and the Holy Spirit share the same deity. At the same time, the Holy Spirit, despite the word "Spirit", is not some vague force (ibid, 879), but a person whom we Christians can form a close and profound relationship with. We have seen, in the Old Testament, that the Holy Spirit was significant in creation (ibid, 882), and in anointing certain people with the abilities to complete God's tasks, such as when Bezalel was to construct and furnish the tabernacle (ibid, 883). And in Jesus' time, the Holy Spirit became even more prevalent in our understanding, with Jesus' incarnate existence (ibid, 885), His ministry and miracles (ibid, 887). The Holy Spirit empowers us as Christians as we move forward in the process of sanctification (ibid, 888). And to some, the Holy Spirit bestows special gifts of prophecy, service, teaching, wisdom, healing, glossolalia[56] (speaking in tongues), and evangelizing (ibid, 891).

---

[56] Glossolalia or the speaking of tongues, is a rare gift bestowed by the Holy Spirit whereby a true believer is able to utter sentences or speech in

In Part 10 (ibid, 901), Erickson discussed the concepts of salvation in the Christian context, which is decidedly different from all other faiths, where a redeemer came to sacrifice on our behalf and in turn provided the salvation for us as believers, through the revelations in His Word.

In the issue of salvation, there is a debate ongoing, on the topic of predestination (ibid, 920). For example, Calvinists would argue that there is unconditional predestination and limited atonement, whereby God has given special favor to the elected, such as the tribes of Israel (ibid, 928). In Calvinists' view, God has irresistible grace and it is this grace which provides the totally depraved humans the limited atonement and for some, predestination. Arminians would still retain the concept of election, although they would argue against unconditional predestination, and believe that foreknowledge of God in persons who would be elected would receive salvation, whereby God knows that some people would receive Christ, and can be elected. The Arminian position argues that if there is a finite number of people who can be saved, as argued by Calvinists, then there is no need to multiply disciples or minister to all peoples (ibid, 934).

God's grace provides the means to salvation, but first, we get a calling from God. He does that through various ways. When someone comes into contact with the Bible, that is God's calling to allow us to study the Scriptures and when we encounter a phrase such as when Jesus said, "Come to me, all you who are wear and burdened, and I will give you rest" (Matthew 11:28), many of us would be moved and will let go of our doubts and fears, and turn to God.

---

a language unknown to us (but intelligible to the audience as a whole). However, there is frequent debate as to the authenticity to some of the claimed glossolalia cases in some charismatic movements (Wikipedia, 2007).

God also works through the Holy Spirit to bring extraordinary personal experiences to pre-believers, and allow them to see the truth and grace of God, and in so, turn towards God. Next, we convert to the Christian way of life, and walk ever forward in a long, arduous process of sanctification (ibid, 946). Along the way, we falter and fall, frequently, and we must repent for our sins and pray for God's forgiveness (ibid, 947). And as we study, pray, and contemplate, we build on our faith in God, by allowing God to worry for the mundane things, as we trust God ever more and more (ibid, 951). God will also regenerate us, by renewing us through a supernatural process of "new birth" (ibid, 958).

One of the mysteries of salvation is our union with Christ. With this union, which is judicial in that God will judge us as a united entity and proclaim, "they are righteous" whereby it means Jesus is righteous and we are righteous (ibid, 965). In a legal context, it is as if a husband and wife shares the communal assets and they are judged collectively together in a financial perspective when judging their collective net worth. Next, the union with Christ is spiritual, since the Holy Spirit resides in us to create this unique and special bond with Christ (ibid, 966). One of the important things to remember is that with this union, we will suffer as disciples (ibid, 967). Christians must not imagine the path of Christianity is a cozy, relaxing path of luxury and comfort, but more of an earnest and sincere attempt of prayer, study, contemplation, and practice. In return, we hope to return to a restored state, in the process of justification (ibid, 968). The Old Testament prescribed a forensic or judicial righteousness whereby justification meant that believers were judged to be free from guilt (ibid, 968). However, we came to realize that God bestows justification when we exercise pious faith and also works.

As Christians, God does not simply leave us alone to try to scale the mountains to reach Him. Rather, He continuously helps the transformative process to allow us to be sanctified in the image of Christ, as we lean and move forward to Him (ibid, 979). God will also exercise His irresistible grace continuously so that we can remain in our faith in Him. Despair and desperation will attempt to falter us now and then, but God will ease away the despairs through His miraculous and sometimes subtle works, so that we as believers can remain faithful (ibid, 996), and ultimately, allow us to be glorified in His name. It is not sheer optimism and hope that God gives, but the fact that in Christ's second coming, we will be perfect and complete (ibid, 1013). One can receive this salvation through the means of receiving, reading, contemplating, and praying through the Word of God (ibid, 1021).

In Part 11 (ibid, 1035), Erickson discussed the entity known as the church, which to different people tend to mean so many different things. The church is not simply architectural in the shape of a cathedral, but much more spiritually. First, a church must have God's people, who are believers. A church must also be the body of Christ, with Christ as the head of the church, as in 1 Corinthians 12:27 when Paul said, "Now you are the body of Christ, and each one of you is a part of it" (ibid, 1047).

On the topic of Israel, Erickson discussed the position concerning the "national Israel" as in the Old Testament, which was a geographical Israel, and the position of the "new Israel", which is wherever God's people are in the form of the universal church. Even though Jews are still God's chosen people, they would need to accept Christ in some point in the future, through God's irresistible grace (ibid, 1053).

Although the Roman Catholic, the Orthodox Church, and the Anglican Church are perhaps the strongest supporter of the view of a visible church as the valid church (ibid, 1054), it does not imply a membership in a visible church means salvation and sanctification in God's eyes. It was said in 2 Timothy 2:19, "The Lord knows those who are His" (ibid, 1057).

The church has some functions in our daily life. It carries out Christ's ministry through the Word of God (ibid, 1069), by evangelizing to disciples and converting pre-believers, providing worship, and fellowship amongst the believers (ibid, 1064). The church also extends itself into secular society through works and social help, showing Christian love and compassion to the greater community at large (ibid, 1067). The church can be Episcopal (ruled by bishops) (ibid, 1081), Presbyterian (ruled by a board of elders) (ibid, 1085), Congregational (democratic and autonomous) (ibid, 1089), and Non-government (whereby they do not have much structure, like Quakers[57] and the Brethren[58]) (ibid, 1093).

One of the most important rites of the church is the sacrament of baptism (ibid, 1098), which is a means of saving grace for a new committed believer. The church also conducts the rite of The Lord's Supper (ibid, 1115) of bread

---

[57] Quakers, or more correctly the Religious Society of Friends, was founded in 17th century England as a Christian denomination dissatisfied with existing Christian denominations then. It is usually credited to George Fox. It seems to be a mystic method and discussed the "inner light" as a way to reach God (Wikipedia, 2007).

[58] The Brethren, or Plymouth Brethren, started in Plymouth as well as Dublin and London, in the late 1820s. The Brethren was called because the members called each other "brother" as opposed to any official title or "rank" within the church. It is an evangelical movement, and John Nelson Darby is also considered part of the Brethren movement, later designated the Assembly movement (Wikipedia, 2007).

and wine, which proclaims our belief and remembrance of Christ, and imparts the sacramental benefit on us believers.

There is some disagreement to what the Lord's Supper means to different denominations, especially in the presence of Christ. The Roman Catholic view maintains that the bread and wine contains fully the body, soul, and divinity of Christ, and that the bread and wine is transformed (ibid, 1125). The Lutherans disputes the transubstantiation view of the Roman Catholic Church, whereby the bread and wine is transformed, but yet the bread and wine contains the body and blood of Christ (ibid, 1125). Martin Luther does agree with the Roman Catholic view that the Lord's Supper is a sacrament (ibid, 1126). The Reformed view differed from both Lutheran and Roman Catholic, and maintained that Christ is present in the Lord's Supper, but not physically or bodily (ibid, 1127).

As all Christians remember Christ through the Lord's Supper, there is also an important element in an attempt to unify the church (ibid, 1135), through ecumenism. There should be consensus to realize that there is but one church, which is the church of Jesus Christ, even as there may be denominational differences. There should be spiritual unity of all believers, through expression of goodwill, fellowship, and love for each other no matter what doctrinal divide there may be (ibid, 1152).

In Part 12 (ibid, 1155), Erickson finished up with the discussion of the Second Coming and the end times. While there may be differing views to when the end times would occur, Christians should be mindful in anticipation for such a future event (ibid, 1171).

Everyone dies at some point, and there is no sense to deny this event for individuals (ibid, 1172). There is physical death, spiritual death, and eternal death. For pre-believers confronted with death, death is a curse and a punishment (ibid, 1177), but a Christian should embrace the dying moment, knowing that it is not an enemy to be feared, but the road to joining God.

The Second Coming is a definite event that will come, with Christ will come in power and great glory (ibid, 1193), but we do not know when that would happen. The Second Coming will see a resurrection of the believers and also unbelievers, and a final judgment with Jesus Christ as Judge will occur, to ascertain our spiritual status, and being final, the judgment of the true believers and the evil will be irrevocable and permanent, and the people sent to the final places, whether heaven or hell (ibid, 1209). In the concept of hell, although there is still debate on how hell is like, we can be certain hell is devoid of the presence of God, and it will be eternal suffering (ibid, 1242). We must also remember that heaven is not about physical enjoyment, but rather, a close proximity to the presence of God, and enjoying that eternal bliss (ibid, 1248).

Top 5 Themes and Why

Erickson's book is a massive textbook but yet tempered with very readable parts and classification. His book is a definite must-read for committed Christians and learning theologians and ministers alike. The top 5 themes that the author found important include these.

First, Erickson's definitions and discussions of what God is like, in his great majesty and yet eternal holiness and goodness, whereby He manifests in the Triune form of Father, Son and Holy Spirit, making Him accessible to all. This is important to evangelize to pre-believers of a loving Deity and one who makes Himself close to our hearts and close in terms of reach.

Second, while humans are inherently flawed with sin, Erickson discussed God's provisions and providence for His children created in His image, and believers. This is important in creating a sense of both humility and yet self-worth, in that we can be sanctified towards God.

Third, Erickson spent a great deal of effort to discuss Jesus Christ our Lord, to ensure that learners understand that Christ's works and sacrifice on our behalf, to redeem us from sin and eternal suffering.

Fourth, Erickson discussed the Holy Spirit and put in perspective various views and Scriptural areas, so that people can grow to understand the third part of the Triune God, a unique feature of Christianity not found in other faiths.

Fifth, Erickson discussed what salvation means to believers in Christ, whereby we can be united with God not just through a simple belief, but through an ongoing system and framework, as well as His Word through Christ's Gospels.

Author's Notes

Erickson's textbook puts light in many questions often left unanswered in the local churches and fellowship groups, perhaps because of a lack of theologians in the local community.

In Asia, where many alternative faiths exist, sometimes for a long time before Christianity is even heard of, a strong theological background especially seen in Erickson's textbook, would be essential for a practicing minister and evangelist to answer many tough questions, and to offer either possibilities or opportunities to pre-believers, to slowly win them over to the Christian path. Erickson's textbook will be extremely helpful for the author to move forward in the future ministries, especially in areas such as Asian countries entrenched with many other faiths, by providing ready answers, alternative views, and very balanced possible views that can be used to explain anticipated tough questions that may be raised by steadfast non-believers not yet won over to the Christian way.

Charismas and Contemporary Changes

Charismas and Contemporary Changes

Abstract

This book is one of many highly regarded books by Professor Philip Rieff, such as "Freud: The Mind of the Moralist", "The Triumph of the Therapeutic", and so on. Rieff abandoned the authoring of this book early on in 1976, disheartened at the lack of theologically-driven morality and values in America, until two of his students, Professor Aaron Manson and Daniel Frank, persuaded Rieff to work on the manuscript of this book again. Manson and Frank subsequently became the editors for the book, and saw the book to completion. Rieff died on July 1, 2006.

A caveat of this book lies in its language, which perhaps either belie its age, or the verbosity of the author. The book will most likely appeal to scholars, philosophers and theologians, and less likely for the average reader.

Rieff's book examined the concept of "charisma", which has changed social meaning from the time of Christ our Lord, to the modern times. In ancient times, Christ stood for the righteous, holy, and perfectly charismatic leader people could look up to, to emulate, and to follow his path. However, Rieff's analysis is that the modern "charismatic" leaders are the exact opposite of Christ, exhibiting none of the righteous, holy and wise attributes we so often lean on with Christ. Rieff saw modern "charismatics" as people with a superficial, "sprayed on" façade of charisma, which has none of the true meaning of the original charisma of Christ. Rieff also examined the gift of divine grace and faith, and how it has been steadily robbed from modern civilizations, and replaced by secular and decadent value systems. To Rieff, denying God's commandments and Word, is robbing all humanity of any possibility of receiving true faith, true wisdom, and grace.

In Part 1 "The Charismatic Foundations of Culture" (Rieff, 2007, 3), Rieff started on a contemplative and perhaps somewhat somber mood, with the postulation that perhaps the notion that there are still charismatic and gifted leaders is but an illusion that has no future. Rieff started with the premise that there can be no charisma[59] without creed[60]. Although most people in the contemporary and secular world would associate charisma to be celebrities, sports personalities, or politicians with personal charm, Rieff believes that this so-called "charisma" exhibited by the contemporary secular personalities are only pretenders. In fact, Rieff even called these people "terrorists" (ibid, 5), in that these people robbed others of the notion of true charisma, as defined as a gift divinely bestowed.

Rieff defined two kinds of people – charismatics, and therapeutics. To Rieff, charismatics are people who hold on to faith and beliefs, and are capable of understanding that there is a God and that God bestows gifts. Therapeutics, in Rieff's view, are people who do not quite believe in God, and use reason and logic to attempt to explain things away.

Rieff took a strong position against Max Weber[61] whom he said, "Weber's entire treatment of religion is utterly suspect" (ibid, 7). Among some of the opposing thoughts, Rieff observed that non-Orthodox thinkers see taboo and prohibitions, as primitive and savage, and therefore unjustifiable (ibid, 13). The liberalists tend to think that laws, ethics and such are confinements and

---

[59] Charisma – 1. The ability to inspire enthusiasm, interest, or affection in others by means of personal charm or influence. 2. A gift or power believed to be divinely bestowed (Encarta World English Dictionary, 2007). Rieff's idea of charisma is more likely the second definition.

[60] Creed – 1. A formal summary of the principles of the Christian faith. 2. A set of religious beliefs. 3. Any set of beliefs or principles (Encarta World English Dictionary, 2007). Rieff's idea of creed is more likely the first definition.

[61] Max Weber (1864-1920 AD) was a German thinker in sociology and public administration. He wrote on religion, faith and Protestantism, among many other secular subjects (Wikipedia, 2007).

perceive them as "irrational", alluding that science has no place for irrational reasoning. However, it remains to be seen that the many scientific thought is evolutionary and remains today, as much of a mystery as centuries ago, and new questions often arise to refute previously thought firm and proven theories.

Rieff then talked about Jews, as the creedal people of God (ibid, 14). However, to Rieff, there are Jews who are disbelieving of their election and charisma by God, such as socialist thinker Karl Marx (ibid, 14). Perhaps, as Rieff thought, the Jews carried a heavy debt of this divine election, since the Jews' election is "a kingdom of priests and a holy people" (Exodus 19:6), something that becomes increasingly heavy to bear as a burden. Also, God's commandments and law runs against common human nature and innate flaws, and so the Jews must have had a tremendous experience, according to Rieff (ibid, 16).

Rieff observed that there is a natural aggression in mankind, with the desire or need for destruction in order to gain power and material goods (ibid, 19). Rieff referenced Søren Kierkegaard[62], who thought that spirituality meant opting out of the fight to be a man of power (ibid, 21). Therefore, spirituality runs against the grain of human nature that seeks to conquer, command and control.

Weber seemed to believe that discipline and charisma are opposing forces, while Rieff believed a strong sense of discipline is an extension of personal charisma (ibid, 28). Rieff believed that Weber, being a modernist and liberal,

---

[62] Søren Aabye Kierkegaard was a Danish philosopher and theologian who argued against the use of excessive ritualistic practices (Wikipedia, 2007).

together with Sigmund Freud[63], were hostile to Christian charisma (ibid, 29). Rieff mentioned that Freud denounced faith as analogous to neurosis (ibid, 29).

Prophets are gifted with charisma, as prophecy itself is a unique gift from God (ibid, 41). However, Rieff mentioned the difficulty ancient prophets had to go through, as many would have denounced the prophets and called them insane. Also, the occasional emergence of false prophets only made the charisma of being a prophet a difficult one. A true prophet is selfless, while a false prophet is self-serving, according to Rieff (ibid, 43). Rieff also saw how some Protestant thinkers strayed away from God, by being too rational and reasoning, rather than simply obey God (ibid, 47). To Rieff, this runs against how a prophet's charisma is bestowed, by simply believing in God.

Rieff also commented that Weber was a scientist, not a Psalmist, and therefore carried both the axe of denunciation and the sadness of science, rather than the grace and strength of a Christian believer (ibid, 51).

Rieff also explained that Jesus Christ our Lord does not possess charisma, since He is God and was not conceived in the same way as we are, and therefore, there was no bestowing of divine grace upon Him, since He is already perfect in every way (ibid, 55). Rieff observed that Christ did not bring cultural achievements such as art and music to the world, but focused only on bringing a method of deliverance and salvation to mankind (ibid, 58). However, Christ's resurrection and ascension demonstrated as practical proofs of charisma, even though He is God (ibid, 59).

---

[63] Sigmund Freud (1856-1939 AD), born Sigismund Schlomo Freud, was an Austrian neurologist and psychiatrist best known for his theories of the unconscious mind and psychoanalysis (Wikipedia, 2007).

Rieff then reasoned that the faith/guilt order of things, whether Christians possess a faith built on the guilt of sins, is an important order of things. Rieff showed that the sacraments of baptism (ibid, 61) and the Lord's Supper (ibid, 62) are affirmations that serve to strengthen the faith/guilt order in believers, thereby binding them together. And Christ's ultimate sacrifice of His perfect good being to bring salvation to the sinners, also serves to strengthen the faith/guilt order (ibid, 63). Rieff also explained that Gnostics and Christianity are decidedly different, inn that Christians depend on the Lord as the highest lord of faith with full obedience and prayer, while Gnostics chase after Christ's deliverance with His secret knowledge. Rieff further said that the Apocryphal gospels and Acts did not achieve canonical status because of their Gnostic elements (ibid, 67).

Rieff explained that obedience to secular authority is very different from obedience to divine authority. Obedience to secular authority may mean simply obeying secular laws that bind by fear of punitive punishment or financial losses, while obedience to divine authority, or charismatic authority as Rieff called it, is about having the faith in this divine authority to derive deliverance and salvation (ibid, 71).

Christians are to not only obey the commandments, but to live in imitation of Christ, which the path is charismatic in nature (ibid, 83; Galatians 2:15-16).

Charismas take many forms. Some of the gifts are extraordinary in nature, such as prophecy and healing. Others are more moderate in nature, such as the gift of teaching and preaching (ibid, 88).

Rieff also warned against fanaticism, where faith is pushed to unrealistic and unsupported realms (ibid, 91). Therefore, fundamentalism and fanaticism can be said to be "possessed by a demonic figure" (ibid, 91), according to Rieff. For some fanatics, their delivery of ideas and beliefs would completely alienate others, including believers and pre-believers alike.

In Part 2 "The Therapeutic Foundations of Anti-Culture" (ibid, 97), Rieff further studied Weber and commented that since Weber was not a therapeutic with solutions to pitch to people, he showed signs of despair (ibid, 101). However, Weber did point out something interesting, in that genuine charisma should not be tied to any political doctrine. The trouble was that charisma was increasingly tied to political leanings in various sectors, and Weber wanted very much to show that true charisma should be utterly divorced from any political threads. True charisma should be transformative in the people whose lives are touched, rather than the false charisma associated with secular personalities.

Augustinian monk Dr. Martin Luther was attributed to the Reformation that brought about Protestantism. Luther affirmed the infallibility of the Word of God, rather than the infallibility of clergy in any appointed office. He said, "In popery, we trusted in the merits of the monks and others; but now each one had to trust to and depend on himself" (ibid, 104). However, Luther was not so fanatical to denounce all rituals and ceremonies if people were accustomed to them, even if they were not mentioned in the Bible (ibid, 105). Luther also showed the way to reuniting man with God once again, by removing the barrier created by the routines and monopoly of the charismas through the Roman Catholic Church (ibid, 110).

Weber did not properly define true charisma properly, according to Rieff's analysis, which then led to Weber thinking charisma can be "value-neutral" (ibid, 124). In Rieff's view, true charisma is value-dependent. At the same time, both Weber and Freud believed that therapeutics are the true dominant types in modern society, and relegated charismatics to less influencing positions (ibid, 125).

Recognition seems to be tied to what true charismatics would look like (ibid, 126). Rieff showed that Jesus did not seek recognition, but rather, attempted to escape recognition. This again contrasts with modern charismatic pretenders, who seem to live and breathe solely on social recognition and rewards. Rieff also mentioned that true charismatics could never make a profession out of being a charismatic, while false charismatics, such as those in politics and entertainment, can (ibid, 136). Rieff also used the analogy of lawyers (ibid, 151). In Rieff's view, modernist lawyers work against the legal framework and authority, if they are the defending end (ibid, 151).

Rieff added that there are much ambivalence in our world, and the balancing force has to be some kind of charismatic or charismatic organization (ibid, 155). Rieff quoted the Christian Church as a model institution of providing a stabilizing force for ambivalences we face. Therapeutics on the other hand, attempt to show people the transgressions of such expressed ambivalences, and then persuade or force people to take action to tackle the transgressions (ibid, 157).

Rieff postulated that true charisma usually occur as a short burst of brilliance and then disappears (ibid, 158). True charismatic personalities seem to appear for a short while, exhibit extreme brilliance in expression and wisdom, and then fade away (or in some cases such as the case of Christ our Lord, died). Thereafter, the principles or expressions of the charismatic will take shape in a charismatic organization, such as the Christian Church.

Modern false charismas are often linked to various transgressions, as Rieff observed, including orgy and narcotics, of dance, rock music, politics, etc (ibid, 176). This again contrasts sharply with true charisma, which springs from a righteous authority as a gift given to believers. Rieff consistently reiterated that political charisma is transgressive, perhaps due to the lack of righteous and holy values behind such arenas.

In Part 3 "The Triumph of the Therapeutic over the Charismatic" (ibid, 191), Rieff lamented that organized belief did not manage to protect people from transgressions more than organized intellect.

As such, Rieff observed that as false charisma obscured true charisma, therapeutics gained prominence, when rather than relying on divine grace and charismas through a lifelong path of faith and prayer, more and more people seem to rely on the methodical and rational techniques of the therapeutics (ibid, 197). Rieff believed that science and politics are both transgressive in nature, and ran contrary to the true charismatic path (ibid, 205).

Rieff explained that compassion must be deeply rooted with a faith/guilt order, with transgressions universally recognized (ibid, 208). When transgressions are no longer recognized universally or even trivialized, and then compassion will die in people.

Rieff saw Weber as a symbolist of anti-charismatic culture, as Rieff observed that Weber could not tell the gift of grace could only be bestowed through "obedience to renunciatory command" (ibid, 225). Rieff quoted Micah 6:8, "Yahweh seeks nothing from you except that you do justice, love faithfulness, and walk humbly with your God'.

Top 5 Themes and Why

Rieff's book required a contemplative and serious read in order to extract his key assertions, since the book is verbose and repetitive in so far as scholarly debate is concerned. Here are the top five themes that the author found useful.

First, Rieff spent a great deal of effort to define what true charisma is, which is a gift bestowed by divine authority. Therefore, true charisma is important for Christians who need a compelling supporting factor to identify with their faith in God.

Second, Rieff debated heavily on false charisma, so evident in personalities throughout contemporary societies, whereby reason, science and politics seem to dominate, rather than God and His Word. This is an important theme because of its realism in a decaying world we live in.

Third, God's commandments and Word are important taboo and prohibitions that are not meant to bind in a restrictive sense, but rather in a liberating way, in that conforming and enlightened Christians who follow God's tough laws will find salvation and liberation. As the Chinese saying goes, "good medicine is always bitter".

Fourth, the concept of faith and guilt going together to counterbalance each other, is instrumental in our Christian path. There must be a strong steady faith coupled with a humble heart knowing we are bathed in sin, which draws us close to our Triune God. Therefore, Christians should recognize that faith and guilt must work together, and a believer should not have one or the other, but must have both with a leaning and focus on God.

Fifth, Rieff's idea that therapeutics have gradually replaced charismatics, is a bitter reminder to servants of the Word to continue to evangelize and reach out to believers and pre-believers, so that God's Kingdom can truly be glorified and exalted. Much more positive energy must be pumped into progressive and forward movement in fighting against the tide of therapeutics.

Author's Notes

Rieff's book is a grim lament that the therapeutics and false charisma is slowly gnawing away at God's true charismatics and their expressions on our world. There remains so much more that needs to be done to defend against the false prophets, the false charismatics, and the therapeutic movement that aims to defeat righteous faith and a trust in God. The author feels strongly that although Rieff took an overarching scholarly approach to this topic, the topic has a very real world feel to it, and demands grave and serious attention from ministers, evangelists and theologians alike. Rieff did not paint a rosy picture, which only served to remind the author, the tough journey ahead.

On Sacraments and their purposes

On Sacraments and their purposes

Abstract

The author explores the basic sacraments and also the distinct differences in implementation and theological thought behind the view of sacraments and ordinances in various Christian traditions, including the perspective of the pre-Nicene traditions.

Sacraments, or sacred actions (Webber, 1993, 79), is an important part of Christian worship that stresses heavily on liturgy, in order to bring believers closer to Christ and allowing us to receive God's grace. The Orthodox Church has, since the early church days, described the sacraments as mysteries (Greek "mysterion"), as the mystery of faith cannot be humanly explained completely.

Two of the more universally accepted sacraments within most mainstream Christian denominations, whether Roman Catholic, Orthodox, Protestant or pre-Nicene (such as Celtic) are baptism, as commanded by our Lord Jesus Christ, as well as the Eucharist (or the Lord's Supper or Holy Communion, as mentioned by St. Paul in 1 Corinthians 11:20), where we commune together in a liturgical worship to receive the blood and body of Christ ascending in our mist through Real Presence of Christ, as often as we can.

Sacraments have evolved throughout the history of Christianity, and as Christian denominations evolved from schism and splits, sacraments began to take on newly interpreted meaning or form. From the early church in the Eastern Greek locales where sacraments were seen as mysterion or mysteries, especially by early church fathers such as Justin Martyr, Irenaeus, Clement of Alexandria and Tertullian. However, they eventually became interpreted as "sacramentum" or new oath by the Roman Catholic Church in Latin, when Christianity spread to the Roman locales (Webber, 80). The Roman Catholic Church also extended the two universally accepted sacraments of baptism and the Eucharist, to include seasonal sacraments such as confirmation, marriage, penance, ordination of clergy (holy orders), and the anointing of the sick. Some denominations also consider the liturgical funeral as one of sacraments.

Today, in some independent non-denominational churches, sacraments seem to have lost a lot of their original meaning of sacred actions with mysteries, and are somehow interpreted simply as acts of devotion to remember Christ, especially in the context of the Eucharist, or the Lord's Supper. Some denominations, such as Anglican, classify some sacraments as ordinances.

St. Paul spoke of the mysteries of God slightly differently, especially in the passages of 1 Corinthians, Ephesians and Colossians, when he relayed mysteries of God is an open and universal instrument for every believer to find salvation, and not just reserved for the elite few (Webber, 81).

Early church father Quintus Septimius Florens Tertuillanus, or Tertullian (Wikipedia, 2007), a noted Latin apologist, described the mysteries as sacraments, where he described as a commitment of believers to God and in turn, receives a commitment from God in the form of grace (Webber, 82). Tertullian explained sacraments in terms of actions of Christ, who baptized, convened in the Eucharist, forgave through the acts of a rabbi, consoled and heal through anointing, incardinated clergy to the church, and anointed holy matrimony (Webber, 82). However, in the example of confession of sins to a member of the clergy, the Roman Catholic Church maintains that as a sacrament, while many reformed or Protestant churches, including the Celtic Church, does not see it that way, as confessions are public, rather than privately to a member of the clergy (Johannine Celtic Christianity, 2007).

The Didache (Wikipedia, 2007), which means "teaching" in Greek, was an early Christian treatise that spoke of rules and rituals for Christian communities, including that of baptism and the Eucharist. It was rediscovered in 1873 and included in the Greek Codex Hierosolymitanus (circa 1053). The Didache was considered by early Church fathers as part of our New Testament, although today, only the Roman Catholic Church retains it as a "collection" within that of the Apostolic Fathers texts. The Didache perhaps gives a hint to the true consideration of mysteries or sacraments, as the book specifically mentioned the two key sacraments of baptism and the Eucharist, as affirmed by all mainstream Christian paths, and especially considering that most of the Protestant denominations only consider baptism and the Eucharist as sacraments.

One of the most important rites of the church is the sacrament of baptism (Matthew 28:19, Erickson, 2006, 1098), which is a means of receiving saving grace for a new committed believer, and be received into the full body of Christ. The Eastern Church calls baptism "chrismation" (Webber, 185).

God's grace provides the means to salvation. However, we first get a calling from God. He does that through various ways. When someone comes into contact with the Bible, that is God's calling to allow us to study the Scriptures and when we encounter a phrase such as when Jesus said, "Come to me, all you who are wear and burdened, and I will give you rest" (Matthew 11:28), many of us would be moved and will let go of our doubts and fears, and turn to God. God also works through the Holy Spirit to bring extraordinary personal experiences to pre-believers, and allow them to see the truth and grace of God, and in so, turn towards God. Next, we convert to the Christian way of life by receiving the sacrament of baptism as commanded by Christ, and walk ever forward in a long, arduous process of sanctification (Erickson, 946):

> "And Peter said to them, Repent, and be baptized, each one of you, in the name of Jesus Christ, for remission of sins, and ye will receive the gift of the Holy Spirit." (Acts 2:38)

The second part of the Didache detailed rules on baptism, which, according to Orthodox Scriptures, must be done "in the Name of the Father, and of the Son, and of the Holy Spirit" in naturally flowing water, such as rivers and streams, the sea, or large lakes. The Didache did provide concessions in the absence of such water, such as using warm or cold water, after an act of consecration. The Didache also mentioned that the clergy and the believer who is to be baptized, and even those in attendance of this baptismal act, should fast for one or two days prior. In the absence of sufficient water, especially that of naturally flowing water, the quantity of water can be simply poured three times over the head during the baptismal process (Wikipedia, 2007).

One of the points of contention in the sacrament of baptism has to be infant baptism (also known as "pedobaptism"), compared to believer's or adult baptism (also known as "credobaptism") (Wikipedia, 2007). The Roman Catholic Church, as with Orthodox, Assyrian, Anglican, Lutheran, Methodist, Reformed and Presbyterian churches baptize infants, while many Protestant branches such as Mennonite, Amish, Brethren, Baptist, Pentecostal, Adventist, Johannine Celtic branches, and non-denominational churches, only practice adult or believer's baptism, as mentioned by St. Peter for people to repent and be baptized (Acts 2:38). Since infants do not have the faculty to express themselves or understand repentance yet, they would be unable to choose to be baptized.

By definition from the Scriptures, baptism in itself confers the full rights and privileges as a new Christian. It should not be seen as a partial act of conversion (Webber, 187). Confirmation follows right after baptism, with an anointing of the forehead and right hand with oil, in the Celtic tradition, while most Protestant traditions may not use anointing with oil. In a Methodist example, baptism is immediately followed by confirmation as well as membership into the church. This act of confirmation is different from say, that of the Roman Catholic Church, whereby the act of confirmation may only take place much after baptism. Most of the Reformed churches reject the notion of requiring confirmation after baptism.

The church also conducts the rite of Eucharist or the Lord's Supper (Erickson, 1115) of bread and wine, which proclaims our belief and remembrance of Christ, and imparts the sacramental benefit on us believers.

With this union with Christ through the Eucharist, which is judicial in that God will judge us as a united entity and proclaim, "they are righteous" whereby it means Jesus is righteous and we are righteous (Erickson, 965). In a legal context, it is as if a husband and wife shares the communal assets and they are judged collectively together in a financial perspective when judging their collective net worth. Next, the union with Christ is spiritual, since the Holy Spirit resides in us to create this unique and special bond with Christ (Erickson, 966). One of the important things to remember is that with this union, we will suffer as disciples (Erickson, 967). Christians must not imagine the path of Christianity is a cozy, relaxing path of luxury and comfort, but more of an earnest and sincere attempt of prayer, study, contemplation, and practice. In return, we hope to return to a restored state, in the process of justification (Erickson, 968). The Old Testament prescribed a forensic or judicial righteousness whereby justification meant that believers were judged to be free from guilt (ibid, 968). However, we came to realize that God bestows justification when we exercise pious faith and also works.

There is some disagreement to what the Eucharist means to different denominations, especially in the presence of Christ. The Roman Catholic view maintains that the bread and wine contains fully the body, soul, and divinity of Christ, and that the bread and wine is transformed (Erickson, 1125). The Lutherans disputes the transubstantiation view of the Roman Catholic Church, whereby the bread and wine is transformed, but yet the bread and wine contains the body and blood of Christ (Erickson, 1125). Dr. Martin Luther does agree with the Roman Catholic view that the Eucharist is a sacrament (Erickson, 1126). The Reformed view differed from both Lutheran and Roman Catholic, and maintained that Christ is present in the Eucharist, but not physically or bodily (Erickson, 1127). However, as we examine the pre-Nicene faith, such as the Orthodox Church (Greek and Russian) as well as Celtic traditions that honor the Orthodox pre-Nicene ways, it would also appear that they agree on the Real Presence of Christ, as identified by early Church father Irenaeus in 180 AD, on the mystery of Real Presence of Christ in the Eucharist where the bread and wine cannot be easily explained (St Andrew's Celtic Church, 2007). This contrasts with the transubstantiation view of the Roman Catholic Church or the consubstantiation by the original Lutheran movement. However, there are signs that the Lutheran movement is increasingly leaning towards the Orthodox Church stance of Real Presence. The Anglican Church has traditionally stood with the Orthodox and the

Reformed view of Real Presence. Some contemporary Protestant movements have relegated the Eucharist to mere symbolism, in remembrance of Christ (Wikipedia, 2007).

The Didache (Wikipedia, 2007) described the Eucharist in Chapter 9, with detailed instructions and prayer related to the cup and the broken bread. Unlike some contemporary movements, the Didache mentioned that the un-baptized, even if they are believers of Christ, should not receive the Eucharist.

Matrimony, ordinary of clergy into holy orders, and the anointing of the sick, as with the liturgical funeral, are considered by some traditions as sacraments, if not at least sacred action (Webber, 273).

Genesis 1:31 does describe the sanctity of marriage between one man and one woman, as a gift from God. Early church fathers such as Clement of Alexandria and Irenaeus (Webber, 274) all proclaimed the goodness of marriage as a gift of God. However, in 1520 AD, Dr Martin Luther taught in the Babylonian Captivity of the Church, that marriage is an institution created by God, but not a sacrament.

The process of ordination into holy orders, was mentioned briefly in Acts 6:1-6, where the chosen were presented to the apostles, who then laid hands on them after completing a period of fasting and prayer. Although ordination rites have evolved since the early Church, especially in Roman Catholic and Orthodox traditions, the fundamental process of laying on hands on the clergy with a prayer, is universal across all traditions, including the Protestant and contemporary ones. Some of the new denominations have also rejected the distinction between clergy and laity (Webber, 305), thereby rejecting the notion or ordination of clergy as a sacrament, by quoting Luther's professions in his 1520 To the Christian Nobility of the German Nation, as saying,

> "St. Peter in 1 Peter 2:9 says, 'You are a royal priesthood and a priestly kingdom,' and Revelation 5:10, 'Through your blood you have made us into priests and kings.'"

The anointing of the sick, especially with oil, is an ancient custom. In James 5:14, James asked the sick to call on presbyters to pray for them and anoint them with oil. The anointing of the sick with oil as a sacramental practice was primarily done for the forgiveness of sin (Webber 332), and in turn, receiving the grace of God through faith and therefore, healing.

One of the rarely practiced sacraments, is liturgical foot washing (Webber, 339), which was spoken of in the Scriptures, such as John 13:1-20, Luke 7:36-50, Exodus 30:18-21, 2 Chronicles 4:6, and so on. The liturgical foot washing was also known during our early Church fathers' time, such as those of Irenaeus, Clement of Alexandria, Athanasius, and Ambrose (Webber, 342). There is a revival of this liturgical practice, whether recognized as sacramental or not, in some Catholic, mainline Protestant, Brethren, (Webber, 343), and some Celtic traditions.

As all Christians remember Christ through the Lord's Supper, there is also an important element in an attempt to unify the church (Erickson, 1135), through ecumenism. There should be consensus to realize that there is but one church, which is the church of Jesus Christ, even as there may be denominational differences. There should be spiritual unity of all believers, through expression of goodwill, fellowship, and love for each other no matter what doctrinal divide there may be (Erickson, 1152).

Constantine and Christianity

Constantine and Christianity

Abstract

How did Emperor Constantine I of the Roman Empire changed Christianity? What were some of the Roman influences that invariably became intertwined with the fundamentals of Christianity? The author explores the changes that Constantine brought about in Christianity through the perspective of the pre-Nicene traditions.

Christianity is not a monolithic stream of thought and practice. It is a rich and varied tradition that has many streams of beginnings. For example, much of the Roman Catholic Church today evolved from the Pauline tradition (from Saint Paul the apostle) with a strong reference to Saint Peter the apostle as the seat (associated with "petra" the rock) and first bishop of Rome, and the Celtic Apostolic Church is a revival of the Johannine tradition (derived from John of Ephesus), which was followed by much of the Gallican, Mozabarec, Coptic and Byzantine churches as well (Dillard, "Johannine Celtic Christian characteristics", 2007). However, in the original Greek text of the Bible, our Lord Jesus Christ said (Matthew 16:18), "kagw de soi (to you, plural) legw oti su (you singular) ei Petros kai epi tauq q petra oikodomhsw mou qn ekklhsian kai pulai adou ou katiscusousin auqs", which meant that Jesus was not referring to Saint Peter as "the rock", but rather, Christ was referring to Himself as "the Rock". He also addressed all the apostles with the power of building God's kingdom (Matthew 18:18), and not just Saint Peter only (Dillard, "Early Church", 2007).

John of Ephesus was a prominent church leader of the Orthodox non-Chalcedonian Syriac-speaking church in the 6th century in Asia Minor (Wikipedia, 2007). As such, the assertions and the liturgy would differ, sometimes quite greatly, even as all streams are unified in the central theme of the Word of God, the Holy Trinity, and our Lord Jesus Christ as redeemer.

While many people, Christians and non-Christians alike, are familiar with the eventual evolution of Christianity from Pauline lines, the Johannine line of thought is less common. However, the Celtic influence was formative even in the early church years. The early Celtic influence, before Christianity set root, was quite prevalent in the Atlantic coast to the Rhine and the upper Danube, as early as 600 BC. The Celtic language spread throughout Western Europe, and by 450 BC, the Celtic culture also permeated throughout northeastern France and southern Germany, although, in Rives' assertion, the greatest influence appeared in Gaul and Britain (Rives, 2007, 74).

Before the bishop of Rome came into prominence in the contemporary world as the steward for Roman Catholicism, Rome and Christianity was not always congruent with one another in history. Christians were known to be persecuted and frequently executed when they professed their faiths before the advent of the fourth century (Rives, 2007, 196), such as the first recorded large-scale persecution of Christians in 64 AD, asserted by historian Tacitus (Wikipedia, 2007). This was because Roman emperors saw themselves as divine, and that was against the principles of Christianity. And for the next 250 years, Christians were to face persecution from the Roman authorities, in many occasions execution, and even the demolition of Christian buildings and homes. The large-scale persecution lessened by 311 AD, where an edict of toleration was issued by Galerius, emperor of Tetrarchy, to allow Christians to practice, although confiscated property were not returned.

With Emperor Constantine I of the Roman Empire converting to Christianity from pagan Roman roots, purportedly due to the influence of his Christian mother Helena, around 300 AD, Christianity became a much stronger religion (Wikipedia, 2007). Some would also claim that Constantine's revelation and conversion came in 312 AD, when he saw a light in the form of a cross in the sky with the words "in hoc signo vinces" or "in this sign you shall conquer", when he asked for Divine intervention before the war at Milvian Bridge. He equipped his soldiers' shields with the cross and subsequently won the war (Wikipedia, 2007). After his victory, Constantine did support Christianity by building large basilicas, granting taxation benefits to clergy, keeping Christian officials in his court, and so on. By 330 AD, Constantine built the Christian-themed new capital, later known as Constantinople.

Constantine I and Licinius issued the now famous Edict of Milan in 313 AD, to remove punishment for professing to be Christians, and also returning confiscated Church property. However, although Constantine became a patron of Christianity, he also invariably caused Christianity and its practices to be infused with various non-Christian ideas, and also that of a centralized governmental hierarchy modeled after his Roman government, quite unlike the apostolic times of Christianity of small communities with de-centralized elders leading believers. For example, in the context of the Celtic apostolic church, the congregation center around individual monasteries, presided over by bishops and abbots, and no bishop is above another. In fact, abbots and bishops share equal "rank" and responsibility, as practiced in the early church such as those that adhered to principles of John of Ephesus (Dillard, "Johannine Celtic Christianity characteristics").

Constantine also presided as arbiter in ecclesiastical matters, as seen when he called several councils to debate on Christian and church matters, such as in 314 AD in North Africa on the Donatist dispute, and in 325 AD during the First Ecumenical Council, or otherwise known as the Council of Nicaea (Wikipedia, 2007). There were also references to Constantine being a supporter or even a believer of the heretical Arian view, evidenced when he reversed the exile of the heretical Arius and banished bishop Athanasius of Alexandria, and also chose Eusebius of Nicomedia, an Arian believer, to baptize him.

The heretical Arius did not believe God the Father and the Son Jesus Christ exist together eternally, and he believed that Jesus was "created by" the Father at some point in time. The Arian view believed our Lord Jesus Christ as "less than" the Father, which obviously ran against the whole central theme of Christology in the form of the Triune God, that of the Father, the Son, and the Holy Spirit (Wikipedia, 2007). Constantine's great influence and power over the Church, including his endorsement of Christianity as a "state" religion, also meant that the idea behind a true separation of the state and the church became diluted, something that also ran against the grain of the Word of God. The Emperor Theodosius I made Christianity the official Roman Empire religion with an edict in 392 AD banning all pagan worship, seemed to have strengthened the Christian path, although again, diluted the concept behind the separation of state and church (Wikipedia, 2007). Theologians are divided on the "Constantinian shift" effect that associated Christianity with citizenship rather than a personal choice to choose God, which would contravene the spirit of holy Baptism. That "Constantinian shift" effect with the divisive new ideas, is still evident today in some countries (Wikipedia, 2007), and would later caused some schism among various schools of thought (Dillard, email, 2007).

In the case of the Council of Arles in 314 AD, it was called specifically by the Donatists on Constantine, to repeal the decision of the Roman Catholic Church under Pope Miltiades (Wikipedia, 2007). The Donatists, led by Donatus, active in North Africa, believed that for believers and clergy who had "fallen away", or renounced their faith and then sought to be reconciled, they could no longer receive the holy sacraments of communion. Donatists also deemed sacraments carried out by clergy who were apostate during those times should be seen as invalid (Wikipedia, 2007). However, the mainline Christianity deemed the Donatist stance heretical, as the purpose of sacraments, such as Communion, was to restore and renew believers. Therefore, the Donatists were condemned by Constantine and the Council of Arles when they convened in 314 AD, and beyond this condemnation of the Donatists and their leader Donatus, the Council also passed various canon law, including the calculation of Easter as a single day only, as well as requiring at least three bishops to consecrate a bishop, which some would say ran contrary to the early Church practices (Wikipedia, 2007, Dillard, "Johannine Celtic Christianity characteristics", 2007).

One of the key problems between the Pauline and Johannine traditions has to do with the calculation of Easter, as well as Christmas (Dillard, 2007).

Easter, otherwise known as Pascha or Resurrection Day, celebrates the resurrection of our Lord Jesus Christ on the third day after his death at the crucifix, sometime between 27 and 33 AD. Traditionally, Easter is linked to the Jewish Passover, which again is linked to the Last Supper between our Lord Jesus Christ and His disciples. Although there was no dispute on the celebration of Easter, there was a dispute to which date Easter should be celebrated, which later came to be known as the Easter or Quartodecimanism controversy (Wikipedia, 2007), which refers to the practice of celebrating Easter on the 14th day of Nisan in the Hebrew calendar outlined in the Old Testament, which was followed by the Johannine tradition (Wikipedia, 2007), also known as Paschal full moon, the first day of the celebration of Passover. The dispute was between the Johannine bishop Polycarp of Smyrna and Rome bishop Anicetus, both of who claimed apostolic authority, when Rome continued the fasting until the Sunday morning, and associated Easter with a Sunday. Although Anicetus became bishop of Rome in 155 AD, the dispute between Johannine bishop Polycarp and Anicetus was not resolved, but they parted in peace (Wikipedia, 2007, "Ante-Nicene Church Fathers"). Polycarp maintained his "14-Nisan" practice as this was the practice of John and other apostles, also stated by early church father Irenaeus and bishop Polycrates of Asia minor in 190 AD, both also adherents of the "14-Nisan" tradition, as with many other bishops in that region in those times.

The "14-Nisan" practice became less and less prominent as the universal church worldwide determined to favor the majority, rather than the lesser community within the Asia Minor region. Since the "14-Nisan" practice was primarily based on the Hebrew calendar and the Christian adherents within the Jewish community became the minority as the gentile church grew exponentially, especially through the Greek and Roman regions and beyond, the then gentile-dominant church seemed to have dissociated itself from the Jewish practices, and by the First Council of Nicaea in 325 AD, especially with the dominant influence of the Pauline tradition within the Roman Catholic Church, the "14-Nisan" practice dropped out of the practice of most Christians. Today, only small communities of "14-Nisan" adherents exist, such as the Johannine apostolic traditions, and some revivalists within the Protestant communities that sought to bring back the Jewish practices.

Christmas is a much more popular and globally celebrated holiday that celebrates the Nativity, or birth of our Lord Jesus Christ. While Easter is not celebrated in many parts of the non-Christian world, Christmas is celebrated in many more countries and observed as national holidays. However, the date of December 25th is also one of contention between the early church and that of the Roman church in the early days (Wikipedia, 2007). The Eastern Orthodox Church observe Christmas on January 6th, because they use the Julian calendar and the Julian calendar is 13 days apart from the Gregorian calendar we use these days.

The period of winter, which was a lull period for agriculture due to colder and harsher climates, became a time for Romans to make merry, relax, and prepare for the new year when Spring arrives once again. Early Romans celebrated the Dies Natalis Solis Invicti, which was the birthday of the unconquered sun, associated with pagan gods such as Elah-Gabal (Syrian), Sol (god of Emperor Aurelian from 270 to 274 AD), and Mithras (Persian), on December 25th (Wikipedia, 2007).

The Catholic Encyclopedia 1908 edition stated, "The well-known solar feast, however, of (Dies) Natalis (Solis) Invicti, celebrated on 25 December, has a strong claim on the responsibility for our December date". The later New Catholic Encyclopedia 1967 edition stated in relations to Constantine circa 250 AD, "Besides, the Sol Invictus had been adopted by the Christians in a Christian sense, as demonstrated in the Christ as Apollo-Helios in a mausoleum discovered beneath St. Peter's (Basilica) in the Vatican" (Wikipedia, 2007). Therefore, it was acknowledged that the choice of December 25th to signify the birth of Christ, and the representation of our Lord Jesus Christ in a manner similar to Apollo-Helios (the sun god), further reinforced the pagan and idolatry origins. Some would also associate the date December 25th with winter solstice, where the sun still shines despite shorter daylight hours, which can be said to be an "unconquered sun". Many early church fathers and theologians would dispute the association of the date December 25th with the birth of Christ, including the likes of Origen (Wikipedia, 2007). The association with emperor Constantine with the winter solstice or Sol Invictus, can be found in three places in reliefs on the Arch of Constantine, and also his official coins bearing Sol Invictus, at least until 323 AD (Wikipedia, 2007). Constantine also decreed on March 7th, 321 AD, the day of the sun, Sunday, as the official day of rest for Romans, which would eventually replace the Jewish Sabbath. The pagan sun religion associated with Sol Invictus, would only cease to officially exist when emperor Thedosius I banned all forms of paganism on February 27th, 390 AD.

So, although emperor Constantine is revered by some traditions as a great Christian monarch, he also invariably created further schism among the early church. Some of the decrees, such as that of Sunday as the official day of rest for Romans, as arbiter to the calculation of Easter, and also the association of Sol Invictus with the birth of Christ, all had ramifications to the later evolution of the church, including the splitting of paths from the Johannine and Pauline traditions.

In any art of diplomacy and negotiation, it would also be common to observe that if two parties take firm stances of adhering to their own views, it would be difficult to "close a deal". So in the light of Christian evangelism, in the context of Asia where many traditional Chinese (or other) families have traditional "pagan" practices or faiths, a gentle introduction to show similarities between Christianity and their faiths would entice them to at least consider Christianity as a philosophy to explore. For example, in Buddhism, Hinduism and Taoism, there is a concept of "karma" or "cause and effect", which would parallel in Christian version of "sow what we reap". In the case of ancient China, the Jesuits were very successful in not only reaching out to the common man, but especially to the Confucian scholars (most of them high ranking court officials) and even the emperor. The Jesuits could achieve this, especially Matteo Ricci, because they sought to understand what the Chinese believed and practiced, such as Confucianism, Taoism, Buddhism, Mandarin language, etc. With an open heart to embrace the Chinese culture, the Jesuits were able to blend in, while slowly converting the Chinese to their faith. They could not have done this if they took the "hell and brimstone" approach many latter day Protestants did. In fact, the Protestant preachers were not as successful in latter day China, because their overzealous ways of branding the Chinese as idol-worshippers and "going to hell" did not bode down well. Cultures are deep rooted, and a need for understanding is especially important. Jesuit Matteo Ricci understood the Chinese were not worshipping idols when they conduct ancestral rites, that the rites were civil and not religious, and that the Chinese were/are simply "honoring their fathers and mothers" as remembrance. In the Philippines, for example, the predominant Christian path is sometimes infused with some pagan practices. In the broad sense, as at least Christianity is in most hearts of Filipinos, which otherwise, would not even exist. There are many ways to find parallels, so that gentiles can slowly understand that Christianity is an acceptable path, and eventually, as they embrace, and get converted (even baptized), they will then seek the path of discipleship and God's grace will point them to orthodoxy eventually. Personally, I use the term "pre-believers" in Asia, as many Asian pastors are beginning to, since this imply they will eventually be united with God, rather than using "unbelievers" or other terms.

Despite such schism, the role of church elders and presbyters are to continue a spirit of compassionate ecumenism, in light of the rising threats to the further and future growth of Christianity, amidst the emerging humanism and secularism of people worldwide. Paganism existed way before Christianity, and so there is no denial that paganism is here, especially in Asia. Paganism exists in time memorial, as man seeks to find the spiritual side, in fact to find communion with God even without knowing it. The means to reach God were and still may not be refined unlike the Christian path, but their hearts yearn to find God, without realizing it. So with the open and ecumenical heart as pastors, the most important thing for ministers of Christ is to gently, subtly, sensitively, and wisely guide pre-believers to embrace God eventually.

Matrimony & Monasticism

Reflections: Matrimony and Monasticism

In the Old and New Testaments

In the early pages of the Sacred Bible, we see in Genesis 1:27-28, "And God created man to his own image: to the image of God he created him: male and female he created them. And God blessed them, saying: Increase and multiply, and fill the earth, and subdue it, and rule over the fishes of the sea, and the fowls of the air, and all living creatures that move upon the earth." And in Genesis 2:24, we have "Wherefore a man shall leave father and mother, and shall cleave to his wife: and they shall be two in one flesh."

Therefore, in the Old Testament, God ordained man to be fruitful and multiply, and that the intimacy between an ordained relationship between one man and one woman was endorsed and sacred. God intended his people to be holy and sacred, to be walking in His ways.

Further, in Genesis 17, we read of God's instructions and decree to give Abraham a son, by ordaining a child from Sarah (earlier Sara'i) his wife. In Genesis 17:19 specifically, our Lord said, "Sara thy wife shall bear thee a son, and thou shalt call his name Isaac, and I will establish my covenant with him for a perpetual covenant, and with his seed after him."

However, not all marriages in the Old Testament were monogamous. There are also instances where polygamy happened, such as found in Genesis 4:19 where Lamech took two wives, one was Adah, and other Zillah. Likewise, the story of Samson and his fall to lust after succumbing to the temptations of Delilah, in Judges 16:15-30, we see that the falling of man to untoward and unordained relations outside that of the marriage of one man and one woman, was obvious.

From the beginnings of the ordained marriage between one man and one woman, to the numerous stories of adultery, polygamy and falling to temptations, we can see the pattern of the Bible in warning us of the ordained form of intimate relations, that of one man and one woman, and those unorthodox forms which should be chastised and discarded. Therefore, the form of sacred marriage between one man and one woman is a necessary step, in the stability of an emerging civilization, and as the formative pattern for future generations, including that of the contemporary world. The instructions for proper matrimony and sexual conduct are appropriately detailed in Deuteronomy, Leviticus, Numbers, and Chronicles. We must also recognize that the proper and sanctioned type of marriage should be observed as a sacred covenant between one man and one woman, with sets of instructions regarding the proper union. It was not a trivial decision to begin with, and should not be trivially ended or interceded in between.

In the issue of virginity in the Old Testament, we see that there is sanctity in virginity, and a man must not defile a virgin and must face the consequences otherwise. For example, Exodus 22:16-17 reads, "If a man seduce a virgin not yet espoused, and lie with her: he shall endow her, and have her to wife. If the maid's father will not give her to him, he shall give money according to the dowry, which virgins are wont to receive."

Symbolically, the Book of Jeremiah also shows that the concept of matrimony need not just be physical between humans, but also, a relationship between God and man, where God can be interpreted as the spouse of man, forgotten and left behind, such as Jeremiah 2:2, "Thus saith the Lord: I have remembered thee, pitying thy soul, pitying thy youth, and the love of thy espousals, when thou followedst me in the desert, in a land that is not sown." In Jeremiah, we also see God's instruction to Jeremiah, in 16:2,

"Thou shalt not take thee a wife, neither shalt thou have thee sons and daughters in this place." This can also be seen as a physical manifestation of our God as the forgotten and forsaken spouse by mankind, and yet with the fidelity everlasting.

From Proverbs 5:1-23, we also observe our Lord showing us the need for matrimonial fidelity in terms of our intimate relationship with God, such as in verse 20, "Why art thou seduced, my son, by a strange woman, and art cherished in the bosom of another?"

And in Malachi 2:10-16 (Darby), we read of our Lord's love for matrimonial fidelity, such as verse 16 which strongly says, "(for I hate putting away, saith Jehovah the God of Israel;) and he covereth with violence his garment, saith Jehovah of hosts: take heed then to your spirit, that ye deal not unfaithfully."

In the New Testament, we see a transition and transformation after Jesus Christ our Lord coming into the picture, where Jesus Christ expanded the mere laws of the Old Testament into the more esoteric and spiritual interpretations of the laws. From circumcision of the Old Testament we have now baptism of the water and the Spirit. From the sacrifices of the Old Testament we now have the Eucharist (or thanksgiving). From the chosen people of Israel in the Old Testament, we now have the expanded world of everyone including the Jews to be saved by the blood of Christ our Lord. We can begin to fathom the older, harsher world of the old Israel, to a more optimistic and hopeful world where everyone can be redeemed by the blood of Christ our Lord. In a nutshell, our Lord Jesus Christ took the old authority of Moses, and superseded it directly with the authority of God Himself.

Our Lord Jesus Christ also expounded the laws of our Lord, on the sanctity of marriage and the sadness of divorce.

When the Pharisees asked Christ about divorce, Jesus Christ showed the hardness of heart of the Pharisees, who quoted Moses allowing divorce of a woman with a mere certificate (Mark 10:4). However Christ said in Mark 10:5-12, "To whom Jesus answering, said: Because of the hardness of your heart he wrote you that precept. But from the beginning of the creation, God made them male and female. For this cause a man shall leave his father and mother; and shall cleave to his wife. And they two shall be in one flesh. Therefore now they are not two, but one flesh. What therefore God hath joined together, let not man put asunder. And in the house again his disciples asked him concerning the same thing. And he saith to them: Whosoever shall put away his wife and marry another, committeth adultery against her. And if the wife shall put away her husband, and be married to another, she committeth adultery."

Jesus, the Son, like our God the Father, was also likened to the spouse in the new covenant He made with man. We find references to invitations to a wedding (Mark 2, 18-19), or comparing the kingdom of heaven to a wedding of the son of a king (Matthew 22:1-10). The Apostle Paul also made references to the spousal relationship between Christ and man, in 2 Corinthians 11:2, "For I am jealous of you with the jealousy of God. For I have espoused you to one husband that I may present you as a chaste virgin to Christ."

Jesus also extended the concept of matrimony and virginity to reach a new and rather novel level at that time, that of celibacy.

This can be found in Matthew 19:10-12, in terms of the possibility of divorce, "His disciples say unto him: If the case of a man with his wife be so, it is not expedient to marry. Who said to them: All men take not this word, but they to whom it is given. For there are eunuchs, who were born so from their mother's womb: and there are eunuchs, who were made so by men: and there are eunuchs, who have made themselves eunuchs for the kingdom of heaven. He that can take, let him take it."

As our Lord Jesus Christ commended, those who can be celibate, should be so. It is a divine mystery that is not for everyone, but for those ordained by God to be so and are free from emotional and physical encumbrances, it would imply that it is right to be so. We also see the Apostle Paul who expounded this concept in 1 Corinthians 7:1-40, on the various sexual relationships between man and woman, and specifically, he mentioned in verse 1 that "It is good for a man not to touch a woman.", if it is so ordained. It can be equated as a high vocation and calling of God, to be bound to God as spouse, with no emotional and physical attachment to another of the opposite sex.

Theologies of the Fathers

If we trace back the times of our Lord Jesus Christ, many of his apostles were married. For example, we saw in Matthew 8:14, Saint Peter, which is the first bishop of Rome, was seen to be married, "And when Jesus was come into Peter's house, he saw his wife's mother lying, and sick of a fever." Yet, if we follow through the passage to Matthew 22:30, we see that our Lord Jesus Christ mentioned that the celibate is akin to angels in heaven, "For in the resurrection they shall neither marry nor be married; but shall be as the angels of God in heaven."

The debate between celibacy/virginity and matrimony has been long standing since the schism of the church universal, even as we observe the early apostles and bishops having had been married. We can see Scriptural references to the virtues of both matrimony and celibacy. However, if we must concede that celibacy is "superior", perhaps it might be better to see why celibacy can work very well and powerfully for those ordained to the celibate life, rather than simply denounce matrimony. It has to do with mental focus of the believer.

For example, many of the revered saints from historical perspectives have been celibate, and perhaps adhered to the strict spousal relationship with God only, rather than split their priorities between God and an earthly spouse and the resultant children from such an earthly relationship. Perhaps we can best explain that God has plans for everyone, and not everyone is ordained to the consecrated life of celibacy. For those ordained to a life of celibacy, perhaps time and energy will be expended in more holistic service to God, than those ordained to fruitful multiplication.

Nowhere in the Roman Catholic Church or the Orthodox Church did it specifically mention that matrimony is a bad thing. In fact, matrimony is a celebrated sacrament in the Catholic and Orthodox Churches, much as it is celebrated in other denominations. Further, Orthodox priests may be married. In fact, it was suggested that the Gnostic Christians and the Encratites[64] found matrimony to be a by-product of the sin of lust, and that liberation could only be found by renouncing lust altogether. In the opposing end, the Roman monk Jovinian[65] suggested that baptism made everyone equal, married or not, and was eventually condemned by the Synods of Roman and Milan in 393 AD. The early church

---

[64] Encratites were heretical Gnostic Christians in the second century who forbade marriage and abstained from meat, and were rebuked by Paul in 1 Timothy 4:1-4 (Wikipedia, 2009).

[65] Jovinian was also branded heretical as he opposed asceticism, by Pope Siricius and Saint Ambrose (Wikipedia, 2009).

fathers also suggested that carnal desire was negative, and that celibacy was a charismatic election of a chosen few by God.

Matrimony does have benefits, as suggested by early church fathers. For example, Saint Clement of Alexandria deemed matrimony equal to consuming food and drink, simply that it should be done in moderation and not indulged. Likewise, Tertullian deemed marriage as a concession to prevent mankind from consuming itself. Origen also defended marriage as the charism of harmony much as it is a worldly reflection of the love of Christ for His church.

How then, is celibacy relevant today? First, we have to recognize that God has fore-ordained everything, including those who are truly of the consecrated life. Second, the consecrated life of celibacy inspires others to recognize that there is an elevated platform of loving God in completeness, and in His service totally without distractions of the secular life. Third, celibacy removes the obstacles many of the laity face in terms of serving many "masters" of materialism, desire, greed, and so on. Celibacy is not a panacea to the ills of the secular life, merely a component of many things necessary to conquer the seduction of the various pretenses and challenges of daily life we face. Celibacy compels one to look inwards, as a form of gravity that many of us who face the daily challenges of the secular life lacks. Many of us have to contend with looking outwards continuously because the distractions and challenges tend to be with us every minute. But if a consecrated life, especially one that encompasses celibacy and a contemplative life, has so few of the worldly distractions and challenges, then it is sensible to presume that such a life would invariably push one to look more inward, and be able to reflect on the relationship with God more intimately.

In the celibacy of a consecrated life, it is important to first establish that the person pursuing the consecrated life is fore-ordained to be totally focused on God and His work, and that such a person is typically devoid of carnal desire. Abstinence by forcing oneself from carnal desire, is one of the main failings of those who have stepped into the consecrated life while still holding fast to desire. Therefore, it is important perhaps, that before a council of senior clergy consider a novice for the consecrated life, some form of contemplative prayer and secular profiling, and an extended period of "testing" this individual, be effected before allowing the novice to take the vows of consecrated life. It is perhaps wiser to be conservative and laborious, when choosing those for the consecrated life, than to be liberal.

So while some churches instituted celibacy in the priesthood, it is also important to know that not everyone is truly ordained or elected for such office within the confines of these churches.

So while the Roman Catholic church determined the consecrated life of celibacy to be a disciplinary requirement of the priesthood, it is not merely a law. For those true to the consecrated life, celibacy must be beyond just abstinence from sexual activity, as seen in 1 Corinthians 7:1-40. Therefore, as a charism, which is so much more than just a virtue, it must imply a pureness of the soul and complete dedication to Christ, whereby we can equate such a relationship as having only a relationship with Christ, and no other. And because such celibacy is a charism, it should be a gift, and not a human discipline of attempting to strive towards a goal (of being celibate). So we can also assume that if one is not ordained and given the gift of celibacy, no amount of human striving will propel one to such discipline. For those who have been gifted with celibacy in the consecrated life, the allegorical intimate relationship between God and man can perhaps be best expressed in

Solomon's Song of Songs, and one to be celebrated as an angelic life.

So then, is celibacy necessary, or mandatory? Perhaps the best answers can be found in the Apostle Paul's message in 1 Corinthians 12-31, where he said that although there is one body of Christ, there are many members. Not all are given the same gifts, but there will be a Divine purpose for everyone within the same body of Christ (church universal).

Laical and Monastic Christian Life

The various forms of Christian life can be found throughout the New Testament. One of the most used verses are the Epistles of Saint Paul to the Romans, such as 5:10 and 6:22. Saint Paul described the fundamental separation of a Christian in any form of existence, compared to a non-Christian, is essentially baptism with water and the Spirit. In the Galatians 3:28, we find one of the most important verses that reaches out to people who are not Jewish in origin, "There is neither Jew nor Greek: there is neither bond nor free: there is neither male nor female. For you are all one in Christ Jesus." Therefore, to the early Christians, there is not much distinction except the fundamental similarity of baptism.

But of course, every Christian would receive individual gifts of grace from God, and is able to exercise such capabilities or live out individual lives in unique ways, rather than homogenous ways. No two person, even identical twins, can exist in exactly the same manner, and live out lives in exactly the same way.

One of the early Church fathers, Origen, who lived before the age of monasticism, gave one of the defining theories of humans. Origen described the human person composed of the body, soul, and spirit. Origen believed that the body is the creation of the molding of mud from the earth into a tangible form, while the soul (or intelligence) is the other creation from God, non-tangible and invisible, and based on the Word of God. The soul is again separated into 2 tendencies according to Origen, the "superior", which is pre-existent and defines the life of virtue, morality, contemplation and prayer; and the "inferior", which is added after the fall and is easily tempted through the body. The soul can have the power of election, whether to pursue the lowly carnal desires, or to pursue the spiritual. The third, the spirit, is a divine and immaterial gift, which is not a constituent of humans.

Origen believed that all rational beings go through 3 states, pre-existence, existence, and resurrection. In pre-existence, all such beings are equal and in divine contemplation with only an ethereal body. After the original fall, such beings would then descend into the existence state and be split into the state of angels, humans, or demons. All humans have both the seed of God and the seed of the devil, and only through resurrection after death can the soul be elevated into the pristine state of divine contemplation and union with God. Origen described vividly, the concept of the internal combat between the polarities of the soul, as a battlefield between the angel and the demon, or between Christ and Satan.

Although the concept of monasticism did not yet exist during Origen's time, his proposition set the tone for the future monastics who sought the separation between the secular and the spiritual, as well as help define the future concept of sacerdotal (ordained priesthood) monasticism. One of the important things to note is that Origen described the Christian life as one that should be dissociated from the world, using the Transfiguration[66] on the mountain as a symbolic representation of going above the world, rather than being in the world.

Origen hypothesized that there are 2 kinds of Christians, simple, or perfect. To Origen, "simple" Christians are those with a rudimentary knowledge of Jesus Christ and the Bible, while the "perfect" Christians tend to have gone through a refining process of discipleship and are supposed to uncover the mystery of Christ in the Word. Origen cautioned such "perfect" Christians to exercise humility.

By the time of Saint Basil the Great, who established Cappadocian[67] monasticism, he defined 80 ascetic rules on his hypothesis of Christian life.

Saint Basil defined the general Christian identity (applicable to any believer) as having these characteristics through the immersion of the Holy Spirit, (1) initiated by faith and energized by love, (2) born or re-born out of baptism, (3) purified of sin through the blood of Christ and enriched by the Eucharist, (4) expressed by living the law of the Word, (5) fellowship of believers, and (6) remaining steadfast to wait for the second coming of the Lord. To Saint Basil, nothing is more important as an expression of Christian discipleship than the expression of love. And this love, which should be pouring towards others, is also demanded towards God, and to Saint Basil, would imply the renunciation of all things that go against God, including

---

[66] Transfiguration of our Lord Jesus Christ can be found in Matthew 17:1-9, Mark 9:2-8, and Luke 9:28-36.

[67] Cappodocia was an area in central Turkey, although the Cappadocian Fathers referred to the philosophers such as Saint Basil the Great, bishop of Caesarea (330-379 AD), Saint Gregory of Nyssa, bishop of Nyssa and brother of Saint Basil (335-394 AD), Gregory Naziansus, Patriarch of Constantinople (330-390 AD), all of whom helped the definition of early Christian theology (Wikipedia, 2009).

much of the defiled world that rejects God's laws. Such was the foundational principle of Saint Basil's proposition of an ascetic or monastic life. Saint Basil defined celibacy as the ultimate expression of the precept of love, and saw it not as a privilege, but a commandment.

Gregory of Nyssa, when he was writing some of his last, attempted to define just what a Christian means. To Gregory, there should not be a "hybrid" life which is an amalgamation of virtue and vice. Rather, life should be absolute, holistic, and a continuance of spiritual pilgrimage and growth. Gregory wrote a paper, "The Life of Moses", in which Gregory saw Moses as an early model for the ascetic monastic.

Athanasius of Alexandria, who wrote the defining work Vita Antonii (Life of Saint Anthony of the Desert[68]), defined the point of the calling of the Lord to the culmination of the ministry, as a journey with an itinerary. To Athanasius, the journey would draw a believer closer and closer to God, and further and further away from the temptations of the world. Athanasius used the paradigm of battles with the demons, more allegorical than physical, to depict that the closer one gets to God, the more powerful and frequent such battles or temptations would be. After all, life is really a constant struggle between the polarities of good and evil within a person, and as one gravitates towards good, the opposing force of evil will become stronger to counter-balance the move, and vice versa. But Athanasius affirmed that only with the grace of God, can the demonic influences, or in this case, temptations, be conquered. And

---

[68] Saint Anthony of Egypt is commonly attributed (wrongly) as the "father of monasticism", part of the Desert Fathers tradition. He is often depicted in the Celtic Cross of Muiredach (Cross of Scriptures) together with Saint Paul, holding up the Eucharistic bread with the Dove (Holy Spirit), signifying the celebration of the Eucharist with the brethren. (Wikipedia, 2009).

grace of God should not be vainly thought of as an insured benefit, so constant prayer and contemplation to beg from God, would be necessary.

Pachomius[69] saw the commonality of monks and laity, in that both shared the sacred commandment of expressing love toward others. However, he believed monks and laity lived out their lives differently. To Pacomius, living as a monk was the ultimate expression of the apocalyptic horizon that awaits, where each day can be deemed to be the last. To Pachomius, forming collective and cohesive monastic communities (koinonia, as seen in Is 43:9), was to become a center where every monk could become the next monk's role model, to spur and inspire each other towards God.

Gregory Nazianzen[70] saw that every form of Christian life can be a life of pursuing perfection. To Gregory Nazianzen, whether one chooses to live a life of chaste matrimony, or one of celibacy, the most important value is humility. Gregory Nazianzen saw the monastic role as one of helping other Christians by illuminating, edifying, and guiding, very much an imitation of the life of Jesus Christ Himself.

An extension of the monastic concept came from Ephrem the Syrian, of Nisibis, Mesopotamia, who wrote "Carmina Nisibena". Ephrem believed that living as a monastic is perfectly compatible with pastoral and apostolic roles, and can be seen as martyrdom without death. Therefore, Ephrem meant that even a celibate monastic can

---

[69] Saint Pachomius is considered the founder of Christian cenobitic monasticism, which stressed a community-led cloistered life, as opposed to the eremitic traditions found in Celtic Christian traditions (Wikipedia, 2009).
[70] Gregory Nazianzen, or Gregory of Nazianzus, was known as Gregory the Theologian, as he was one of the instrumental theologians who helped define the Trinitarian theology widely accepted today (Wikipedia, 2009).

exist perfectly in the world, without necessarily living alone and away from the general population. This concept became a common phenomenon today, with many monastics who are also priests who preach and perform liturgies to the general population.

Cassian, who wrote 2 important works on monastic life, "Instituta coenobiorum" and "Collationes", saw the monastic life as a symbolism for being crucified for the world and living martyrs, which can also serve the greater community at large for the long haul. On the issue of living martyrs, Cassian mentioned 3 forms of monastic life, cenobites, hermits, and sarabaits. Hermits live according to God's will, alone. Cenobites too, live according to God's will, but in a cloistered community. Sarabaits differ from cenobites and hermits, in that they live within their own personal houses but do not conform to the rule of poverty and obedience, and work to secure their future.

While some may describe sarabaits as "unfaithful" (such as author Fr. Domingo Molero cmf who hypothesized that sarabaits do not follow the rule of poverty and obedience), in that sarabaits do not live as cenobites and hermits, sarabaits as a contemporary and Protestant ministerial form is not uncommon, as witnessed in the form of bi-vocational ministry. In the contemporary world, bi-vocational ministry is becoming an emerging trend, due in part to the changing economic conditions where some smaller parishes (such as Protestant) no longer have the ability to provide stipends or remuneration for their clergy, as well as an increasing importance to immerse Christian apostolic and evangelical ministry into the marketplace. However, there is an unwritten rule that bi-vocational clergy should find work that is not contradicting to the Word or their apostolic and evangelical ministry. Also, contemporary "sarabaits", although not adhering strictly to the rule of abject poverty, do not necessarily cling to wealth and materialistic items. Also, such ministers may still adhere to the rule of obedience to a superior (such as a bishop). Some theologians who studied the works of Cassian and his monks, supposed they were semi-pelagians, because they seemed to attach more importance to human efforts and mechanical techniques, rather than the prize of grace and justification.

John Chrysostom saw monasticism as an effective road to spirituality, but does not discount the many obstacles and temptations of such a life. Chrysostom did not see celibacy as the only means to spirituality, but recommended it. To him, staying away from people would have been difficult to manifest the first commandment of Christ, that of expressing love and compassion towards others.

Evagrius Ponticus, a Christian ascetic, who was agreeable with the doctrine of Origen, also saw the need for purification, through apatheia or impassibility, which is to become aware (gnosis) of God so that one can return to the pre-existent state (before the fall). Apatheia can be interpreted as "without passions", and since God alone is free from passions, while demons are full of passions. So apatheia must come from God. Evagrius saw the contemplative path often found in monasticism as a "cure" to lead one to gnosis.

Augustine of Hippo, lived as a monk when he presided as the bishop of his early Christian community of lay-monks. Augustine believed that living as monastics imitated the early Christian community at Jerusalem, which was to be "a community of one heart and one soul, putting everything in common and being provided by the superior according to respective needs." Such a simple life (Acts 4:32-35) was the epitome of an uncomplicated life, quite radically different from the hurried and busy life of today's individual or communities at large.

Like Augustine of Hippo, Caesareus of Arles was also a bishop who lived as a monk among a cloister. He wrote the famous rules of "Regula monachorum" (short rules) and "Statuta sanctarum virginum" (statutes for sanctified nuns/virgins). To Caesareus, he simplified life in the church into just 3 states – virgins, widows, and married people. Caesareus also proposed that matrimony and its sexual relations are merely to have children. However, Caesareus perhaps did not understand Jesus' intentions and teachings with regards to matrimony and God's intent for harmonized joy and blessings, as Caesareus seemed to have extracted his rule for virgins and widows from the New Testament while he extracted his rule for married people from the Old Testament. Therefore, his hypotheses skewed towards believing only celibacy or monasticism leads to spiritual perfection, rather than the universal foundation that a good Christian is simply one who fulfills the commandments, and the completion of the old law through the mysteries of the Beatitudes as taught by Jesus Christ our Lord. In fact, he encouraged the secular laity to look at monasticism longingly as the only path to spiritual perfection. Caesareus also defined female monastic life, with the eschatological and apocalyptic perspective that nuns are supposed to wait for the coming of the Spouse.

One of the distinguishing marks of occidental monasticism is the establishment of rules. One of the basic and most tenets is obedience to a superior, typically the abbot or bishop (or mother superior in a nunnery). Another important virtue is charity, which was described by Abbot Macarius in his Rule of Macarius, when he managed 5,000 monks. One interesting perspective of Abbot Macarius is that his concept of obedience was not unilateral obedience (to him as superior), but rather, mutual obedience to each other in the cloister, as an expression of mutual love.

One very apt description of the monastery is that of "workshop", where God's commandments are fulfilled through a refining and continuing spiritual process. Likewise, the monastery can be likened to a school for learning.

The Rule of Saint Benedict is one of the most defining rules of monastic orders. Other than describing the monastery as school, workshop, of house of our Lord, Saint Benedict also defined the process of the election of the abbot by the community, out of the cloister of brothers. The Divine Office (or "opus dei"), a combination of prayer and contemplation, keeps the monks within the monastery in a consistent and continuous prayer throughout the day. "Ora et labora" is the simple and yet elegant expression of prayer and work for the monastics who uphold such a Rule of Saint Benedict.

On Discipleship

On Discipleship

Abstract

Respected theologian Dallas Willard, in his book "The Great Omission: Reclaiming Jesus's Essential Teachings on Discipleship", talked extensively about the concept of Christian discipleship. Discipleship is increasingly an important journey for any serious Christian, and the author found Willard's book very enlightening in unraveling some of the action steps and thought processes that a Christian can learn from, and adapt to daily journeys.

Willard started by asserting that the word "disciple" appeared 269 times while the word "Christian" only appeared 3 times in the New Testament (Williard, 20). All too often, it would seem that contemporary Christianity, at least in the form practiced or perceived in the corporate church, the word and the underlying meaning behind discipleship is lost. As Christians, we must remember that first and foremost, we are disciples, on a lifelong journey, and that merely getting doused with water during baptism or waking up to the alarm every Sunday and dragging physical bodies to the church building, do not make us Christians. Willard lamented that many Christian institutions seem to have made discipleship optional.

Willard reminded us of the Gospel, that Jesus stressed that his disciples should make disciples of all nations, without regard to ethnicity or backgrounds (Matthew 28:19), which we know as the Great Commission. However, Willard realized that in today's church, it would appear to be degraded to simply making "converts" and baptizing them into "membership". That's what Willard meant by the "Great Omission" (ibid, 23).

As ministers, it is relatively simple to bring pre-believers into the corporate church, and persuading them to become converts. It may even be relatively easy to persuade the converts to remain with the regular Sunday service over a long time, as many large churches have done successfully.

However, the real issue is if such converts then go on to find the true meaning of life, and what it truly means to be a disciple, that equates and mandates a life-long cycle of training, reading, contemplation, and practice. Williard quoted Dietrich Bonhoeffer's 1937 work "The Cost of Discipleship", which attacked "easy Christianity" and "cheap grace". The same sad phenomenon attacks us today, with the onslaught of multimedia, media influence, and decaying humanity (ibid, 27). John Wesley once said, "I must preach law before I preach grace" (ibid, 240), demonstrating the importance of the Law rather than simply stressing on grace, when persuading people to believe in Christ.

Willard added that some heresy has steeped itself into modern Christianity, whereby it would appear some Christians believe (genuinely or otherwise misled into) that as long as they accept Christ, they do not necessarily need to obey Christ as long as they want to (ibid, 36). Willard used the term "vampire" Christians to describe this belief.

Why then, is discipleship important? Much as baptism opens the door to our eternal life, the journey of sanctification through discipleship is the long and arduous process of cleaning ourselves from inside out. While the ancient Pharisees controlled or managed their external behavior well to conform to the Law, Jesus wanted to show us a much more innate and powerful path, that of walking the tough road of discipleship, with the hidden and inner person of us, sanctified from within, so that not only is our outward behavior conforming to the Law, but our thoughts are cleansed and pure as well. It won't be easy, but that's the idea behind Jesus' sermons to His disciples, and for His disciples to pass on to future ones, including us (ibid, 38).

Willard probed our thinking, to asked us as Christians, if we belittle Jesus. Willard was surprised to find many people imagining Jesus only knowledgeable about the Word of God, and yet would not believe that Jesus, the Son, would be all knowing, of everything from the esoteric sciences, to the finest arts (ibid, 43). Why shouldn't Christ our Lord be the master of all sciences, be it astronomy, physics, biology, organic chemistry, medicine, and the like? Why shouldn't He be the greatest of all artists? After all, the premise of all things beautiful we know, must be from God. The rules that govern all things, such as sciences, must be from God. Jesus was thought of by the ancient believers, to be one "in whom are hidden all the treasures of wisdom and knowledge" (Colossians 2:3), so wouldn't that assert Jesus' mastery over all domains of knowledge? (ibid, 44). As professing Christians, only when we completely trust and believe in Jesus and His all-knowing knowledge, can we truly enjoy the relationship with Him even in our secular lives.

One of the most powerful sanctifying factors in our lives, must be the surrender of ourselves to the Holy Spirit (ibid, 55). With the Holy Spirit, we slowly begin to take on the form of our Lord, in that the Spirit distills our inner selves to be walking closer to God, and away from sin. The 9 attributes of a Spirit-filled life must be "love, joy, peace, patience, kindness, generosity, faithfulness, gentleness, and self-control" (Galatians 5:22-23).

Next, Willard discussed the issue of the Sabbath (ibid, 65), which many seem to forget, or ignore. The Sabbath, in Willard's assertion, is a way in which we let God take over and take care of our lives, and in our complete faith in God's providence. The Sabbath also allows us to drop the mundane secular work, and take some time to contemplate in solitude, to communicate with God.

Willard also questioned the charismatic movement, in which some Christians believe that by "some sort of lightning strike of the Spirit", believers will have their personalities and heart transformed and revived (ibid, 88). Of course, we know that cannot be so, as Christian discipleship is a long drawn, dedicated, disciplined, intentioned, painful process, of drawing ourselves closer to God as we believe and apply ourselves, as the Sermon on the Mount taught us. There is NO short cut.

Willard has an interesting point. In today's reliance on computers, personal digital assistants (PDAs), calculators, cell phones and the such, the concept of memorization seems to be taking a back-seat (ibid, 91). However, Willard believes that it is essential as a disciple to take to memorizing the Bible as much as possible. It is difficult, but by memorizing key passages in the Bible, it may possibly get us out of trouble and sin, at critical moments.

Willard talked about grace, and how best to find grace in our lives. To Willard, the best way to have consuming grace, as he put it, is to lead a holy life (ibid, 96). Conversely, what Willard meant was a sinful life would be one lacking in grace, with lots of suffering. In Willard's theology, there is no such thing as grace without a dedicated and disciplined effort to lead a pure life in God's eyes. In Willard's view, "grace is opposed to earning, but not to effort" (ibid, 120). We should remind ourselves of this, "Why do you call me 'Lord, Lord', and do not do what I tell you?" (Luke 6:46).

Spiritual formation is not just something the Roman Catholics would practice, but a path to lead to a life in imitation of Christ, for any Christian. In Willard's view, many modern churches lack a structured method to guide believers into dedicated disciples. However, Willard also warned of having too much rigid structure in a path of spiritual formation, which can lead to exactly the legalistic paths Jesus warned His disciples about (ibid, 116). Willard discussed that spiritual formation should be having both psychological and theological understanding of a good spiritual life. In Willard's view, simply having theological understanding, or psychological understanding, would not help in spiritual formation (ibid, 118).

As students, we must recognize that our flesh is in constant battle with our spirit (ibid, 127). That is not to say that for some, their flesh and spirit could act in tandem to yearn for and seek God. Therefore, it is important for us to discipline our flesh, so that our spiritual yearning for God is united in flesh and spirit. Yet Willard reminds us that just because we are baptized into Christ, it does not automatically transform our flesh to be in unison with the longing for God in our spirit. The unified flesh and spirit transformation is not common, though not impossible either. But we must recognize that we cannot be complacent or conceited enough to believe automatic transformation and unification of our flesh and spirit will take place as long as, or as soon as, we receive Christ into our lives. A classic example would he Jesus' own apostles who readily denounced or ignored Him at the time of danger, even as they genuinely believed earlier they would do no such thing (ibid, 134).

One of the admired saints, Saint Francis of Assissi, is much loved and talked about (ibid, 140). Yet, Willard realized that not many would carry the same passion and discipline of Saint Francis, or emulate his behavior, deeds, and spirit, in pursuit of a holy life. Willard attributed that Saint Francis, or Martin Luther, or John Wesley, can be said to possess a "certain something" that made them different from many of us. Willard also pointed to secular environments where the original founders of organizations may have noble ideals and integrity, but latter day managers ruined the organizations through an obsession with material success (ibid, 141). Willard basically hinted at the difficult of longevity of a noble and holy life. It is easy to believe or even be baptized, but the true measure of a disciple or a minister, is if such a person continues the journey of sanctification right up to the death bed. Staring with a "bang" is relatively easy, but do we continue the journey? Or more importantly, do we also end with a "bang"?

Willard made an interesting observation, that servants of God sometimes relied on their own human wills, to simply be "nice" to the people they minister, without resorting to the spiritual meaning behind the Great Commandment, "Love the Lord your God without all your heart, and with all your soul, and with all your strength, and with all your mind; and your neighbor as yourself" (Luke 10:27). The spiritual love of agape, is perhaps the only form possible for ministers to truly minister well and yet love his congregation for the long haul, without losing heart and patience. In a nutshell, Willard advised fellow ministers that it is important for them to tend to their spirits, in communion with God always, and placing God always in front, in order that they can enjoy the flourishing of agape for the ministers' people. After all, it is through God's blessing to be a minister, and a blessed path demands a constant communication with God the provider.

Some of the recurrent themes, or practices, that Willard talked throughout his book, were "solitude, silence, and fasting". Willard demonstrated that silence and solitude are not easy to contend with, with many modern people failing to find peace in their own space (ibid, 301). A minister should find time always for solitude and silence, away from the hustle of life, especially in today's busy and cruel cities (ibid, 200). A minister cares for the soul of his people, and yet, often, he may well forget to tend to his own soul. In moments of solitude and silence, the minister can contemplate, meditate and pray, and through such moments, be recharged for further service to God. Fasting is not that often practiced, though it would be good, in Willard's view, as it is a formative discipline that helps our soul be more independent of desires of the material world (ibid, 230).

Willard helped to clarify the view of the Lutheran concept of "priesthood of the believer" (ibid, 242). While some evangelical or charismatic streams would take it to mean anyone can conduct priestly duties, Willard argued that is not the case. Rather, any Christian disciple would automatically become an "ambassador" for Christ, and his behavior and patterns would help to solidify more believers, or turn people away.

Willard described the importance of a minister, much as the complete wisdom and knowledge of Jesus did, to have some knowledge of the secular fields (ibid, 279). Willard quoted John Wesley as saying, "Some knowledge of the sciences also, is, to say the least, equally expedient." (ibid, 279). It is useful for a minister to be able to understand the nuances, concerns, realities, of his congregation, by understanding some of the secular knowledge. And besides the empathy of a minister for his people, it is also useful to understand the secular knowledge to be able to draw in real-life examples to use as tools and tactics to persuade people to Christ.

Willard went on to study Saint Teresa of Avila, one of the favorite saints of Catholicism (ibid, 294). Willard mentioned that Saint Teresa said, "considering our soul to be like a castle made entirely out of a diamond..." (ibid, 295), so that our spiritual innate side of us can be unraveled or unveiled, and that eventually, by living a life in imitation of Christ, that inner sanctified side will emerge.

Willard ends his book with some parting wisdom. He warned ministers against the conversion of people of the world, or even the church. Rather, he stressed the importance of a minister in converting himself (ibid, 318). All great conversion and evangelism has to begin with oneself, Willard asserts. The minister must start and continue his life as a disciple of Christ, not merely a "Christian". Then, he can have the anointing of God to make disciples of others. And then, the "great omission" can become Christ's command of the Great Commission.

Showing the face of God in the East

Showing the face of God in the East

Abstract

Jesuit priest Matteo Ricci (1552 – 1610) was one of the most successful evangelists to preach and evangelize Christianity to ancient China, when he was first sent to China in 1582. Christian clergy who came after him did not seem to enjoy as much success as he did. Why?

Matteo Ricci started learning the ancient Chinese language (a much more complex and esoteric script compared to contemporary Chinese) in 1582, and he mastered Confucian classics and Chinese philosophy. He was able to successful blend in Christian theology with the highly developed Chinese philosophies and court bureaucracy, so that he could convince the Emperor and the Chinese people, of the salvation in Christ.

Therefore, given that many "old" cultures exist, some of which predate the New Testament and the salvation in Jesus Christ, it is important to understand the development and use of expedient means to evangelize and educate the gentiles in the greater Asian region, even in the modern world today. What's more, in certain geographies where religion was once curtailed due to certain ideologies, it is important to be able to demonstrate co-existence while providing the means to salvation.

The author will attempt to show how the Jesuit priest Matteo Ricci's ability to transcend Christian evangelism by merging philosophy with Christian theology, while remaining true to the core of Christian thought and orthodoxy, can help to save more souls, rather than alienate complete and large cultures altogether. This can be equally applied in the contemporary context with many disparate cultures, ideologies, and even the advent of technology and science against classical religious thinking. The author does not take a denominational stance, but rather, attempts to demonstrate useful methods and approaches that may be useful in gaining disciples in Asia.

Christian influence in China

The author's research interest is in ministering to the gentiles in a contemporary Asia Pacific, where diverse cultures and pre-determined local religions and faiths can make Christian ministry more challenging. Therefore, the author seeks to find a bridge between traditional Asian philosophy and orthodox Christian theology, by studying how examples such as Jesuit priest Matteo Ricci succeeded in bringing Christianity to ancient China. At the same time, it is the humble belief that every human being has a spiritual yearning towards God, whether or not he or she has the blessing to get to know God, and to embrace His truth. This is manifested by the innate moral laws humans observe or their conscience submits to, as well as their lifelong quest towards finding the truth, the light, and perfection.

The difficulties of evangelizing in Asia

Even as some parts of the world are strongly influenced by Christianity, there are many parts of the world that are not yet blessed by it. Saint Paul reminds us that, "There is no Jew nor Greek; there is no bondman nor freeman; there is no male and female; for ye are all one in Christ Jesus" (Darby, Galatians, 3:28). Therefore, there is an obligation for ministers to minister and evangelize even in difficult parts of the world where Christianity is not yet far reaching, such as many parts of Asia. When we say "gentiles", who are pre-believers, we can be reminded that gentiles are not individuals, but large groups, as derived from the Latin word "gentes", which is the plural form of "gens"[71], which is a clan or group of families.

---

[71] Gens, and plural gentes, is a Latin word describing a clan, caste, or group of families that share a common name and a belief in a common ancestor (Wikipedia, 2007). For example, the Chinese has many

Christianity is facing a tremendous challenge today, simply because there is much more knowledge of it, though sometimes not sufficiently enough to qualify as true faith. Even with the best of intentions of ministers and deacons, sometimes the congregation may have other personal agenda that yearn for pacification, rather than simply follow the Word of God, and live in imitation of Christ. Among fellow ministers, one of the laments the author frequently hears is how difficult it is to reach out to people, especially younger people, these days.

Even harder is that Christianity is an "alien" or "foreign" religion not indigenous to Asia, especially with many Asian nations predating many others in the world, with their own unique cultures, languages, cuisine, and certainly, religions. However, even as the Asians are gentiles who are not native Jews of God's people, Christianity is for everyone. We are comforted by this wonderfully said passage where Jews or gentiles alike share their salvation through Christ, "We, Jews by nature, and not sinners of the nations, but knowing that a man is not justified on the principle of works of law nor but by the faith of Jesus Christ, we also have believed on Christ Jesus, that we might be justified on the principle of the faith of Christ; and not of works of law; because on the principle of works of law no flesh shall be justified" (Galatians, 2:15-16).

As an anecdotal example, according to Census 2000, out of about 2.5 million residents in Singapore, 42.55 were Buddhists, 14.9% were Muslims, 14.8% were with no religion, 14.6% were Christians, and the rest of the

---

different common family names, such as "Phan", or a dialect group, such as "Hakka", "Cantonese", "Hokkien", or "Teochew". In the context of "gentes", therefore, those Chinese sharing a common ancestry and family name can be said to be the same "gentes", while if you expand that context larger, all those who speak the dialect "Cantonese" can be said to be the same "gentes".

population were Taoists, Hindus, Sikhs, and so on (Wikipedia, 2007). The Wikipedia entry also pointed out that the majority of the Chinese population was a mixture of Mahayana Buddhists, Taoists, and Confucianists, with a rising trend of conversion to Christianity.

In other countries, where there is a dominant religion other than Christianity, it would be even more difficult to evangelize Christianity. For example, countries that are predominantly Islam include Malaysia, Brunei and Indonesia, while Thailand would be predominantly Theravada Buddhists, together with quite a few other neighboring Indo-China nations. The Philippines is unique in that it is predominantly Roman Catholic.

Given the bountiful opportunities to evangelize to pre-believers, we are reminded that Christ said, "The harvest is great and the workmen are few; supplicate therefore the Lord of the harvest, that He send forth workmen unto His harvest" (Matthew, 9:37-38). The role of evangelists and ministers are important, as they are diplomats or emissaries of Christianity, the first human contact with pre-believers and a tool for God to allow Him to reach out to many pre-believers who may not yet have the blessing and opportunity to learn about God, and to live in God's Word.

Some of the common evangelistic methods may be perceived by pre-believers in Asia as too aggressive and intrusive, and have failed. For example, some evangelists, perhaps over-zealous in their approach, usually preface their evangelism that only Jesus Christ will save, and those "unbelievers" will go to hell unless they convert to Christianity. This aggressive "hell and brimstone" stance is often too repulsive by pre-believers of other faiths in Asia, and can even cause conflict, and in some locations, may result in even more problems than just verbal conflict.

There has also been instances of denominational prejudices in some minorities from the highly evangelistic and charismatic preachers which, instead of combining the collective strength of Christianity to present to pre-believers in Asia, cause more rift and misunderstanding to pre-believers, and also causing rift with other Christians. This rift is not beneficial to the building of God's kingdom in a rather diverse cultural mix of Asia, and can only serve to complicate the evangelistic field further, since pre-believers may become more confused by the narrower denominational differences, rather than simply believe in the whole kingdom of God.

Therefore, there is a need to find a more amicable, diplomatic, and ecumenical method to approach the issue of evangelizing to pre-believers in Asia. One of the valuable lessons we can learn from is the Jesuit priest Matteo Ricci, who was very successful in evangelizing Christianity in the Ming Dynasty, China. We can learn from his methods and approaches, and others after him, as well as some contemporary suggestions from the author, based on his fieldwork in the corporate world. The author does not lean towards or show preference in any denominational difference, but rather, take an ecumenical approach that seeks to show the useful methods Jesuit priest Matteo Ricci employed during the Ming Dynasty in China.

There is a caveat, which the author recognizes. In the complex legal and social climates in Asia, there is also a need to recognize and accept that there will be pre-believers who will never seek to learn about Christianity, much less embrace it. Therefore, the author prefaces with the disclaimer that while God's salvation is graciously given to all, not all will accept God, given the free will of humans to exercise. Therefore, amongst pre-believers, there will be some who have questions, or are curious about Christianity, and these will be the specific target audience which this paper aims to address and hope to reach with a genuine heart, and not those who have no interest whatever, and will never seek to learn about Christianity.

The author is reminded and inspired by the Lord's assurance to Moses, "And now go, and I will be with thy mouth, and will teach thee what thou shalt say" (Exodus, 4:12). If the intentions of a minister is true to the Lord, and his compassion for pre-believing communities is genuine, the author believes that the Lord will provide divinely compelling means to help the minister to reach out and move even the coldest and the most skeptical hearts.

The Nestorian influence during the Tang dynasty

China attracted many Christian missionaries throughout the dynasties, but the Tang dynasty, around the first millennium AD, was perhaps one of the more prominent times (Gelber, 2007, 50). The early Christian influence at that time was Nestorian Christianity (Aikman, 2003, 35). Nestorian Christianity[72] was founded by bishop Nestorius of Constantinople (Gelber, 51), but was outlawed as heretical in the West by the Council of Ephesus in 432 AD. Nestorius opposed the Orthodox Church by denouncing that Virgin Mary should be known as "mother of God" ("Theotokos"), but rather, should be called "mother of Christ" ("Christokos") (Nestorian.org, Internet, 2007). Nestorius also expounded that the human and divine nature of Christ was not united in one person, as the Orthodox Church taught, but rather, in separate entities (Aikman, 35). The Nestorian movement is still active in

---

[72] Nestorianism is the doctrine of describing Jesus Christ as two persons, the mortal human Jesus, and the divine Son of God, rather than a unified person described in mainstream Christianity. Nestorius, bishop of Constantinople, taught the doctrine (Wikipedia, 2007. Nestorian church, nestorian.org, 2007).

some parts of the Middle East today, now known as the Assyrian Church or Church of the East, with several hundred thousand members.

The Nestorian priest Alopen built the first Nestorian church at Xian, China, in 638 AD. Emperor Gaozhong subsequently awarded Olopen the official title of "National Priest", which meant that Alopen would provide all religious counsel to the Emperor Gaozhong. Such an honor was unheard of before, and usually traditionally awarded to either Taoist or Buddhist clergy throughout the entire Chinese history. The Nestorian influence reached its peak around 790 AD, with six bishops and nine monks. Subsequently, the Nestorian influence diminished when it was banned in the later years of the Tang dynasty, although even by 870 AD, an Arab traveler claimed to have seen a lot of Nestorian Christians at the fringe of China, around Kashgar (Gelber, 50).

Matteo Ricci's success during the Ming dynasty

Christianity and its influence resurfaced again much later after two centuries, after the fall of the Tang Dynasty and the subsequent arrival of the Ming dynasty, this time through Orthodox Christianity in the form of Roman Catholicism. The most successful Christian missionaries were the Jesuits (or Society of Jesus)[73], founded by Saint Ignatius Loyola[74], in 1540 AD, as a form of counter-

---

[73] The Society of Jesus is a Catholic Order, whose motto is "Iesus Homini Salvator" which stands for "Jesus, Savior of Mankind". They were also known to be "counter-reformers" of the Roman Catholic Church, to counter the reformation brought about by Protestantism (Wikipedia, Internet, 2007) (Catholic Encyclopedia, Internet, 2007).
[74] Saint Ignatius of Loyola (1491-1556 AD) was the founder of the Society of Jesus, and the followers were known as the Jesuits (Wikipedia, 2007).

reformation to the Reformation movement by the father of Protestantism, Dr. Martin Luther[75], an Augustinian monk.

Saint Francis Xavier[76], a renowned Jesuit priest, was the first to bring Christianity to Asia, with great missionary success in Japan. Saint Francis Xavier then wanted to minister in China, but unfortunately, died in 1552 before he set foot in any part of China (Gelber, 101). Superior Alessandro Valignano[77], who came to Macao in 1577 with forty-one Jesuit priests, then carried on his dream. Superior Valignano understood that the Chinese were a proud people; and to evangelize Christianity to a proud and established people would be impossible. So instead of trying to force the Chinese to believe in Christ, he told his own Jesuit priests to accommodate culturally to all things Chinese (Wright, 2004, 85).

The Chinese became attracted to the Jesuit priests, who were learned and wise, and so many scholars and government officials, who formed the upper echelons of Chinese society, took to listening to the Jesuits. Valignano

---

[75] Dr Martin Luther (1483-1546 AD) can be considered the starting point of the Protestant movement. Luther switched from legal studies, to theological studies, and completed his doctoral work at the age of 28. While teaching at the University of Wittenberg in 1517, Luther was said to have nailed his proclamation document, the "95 Theses" (CRTA, Internet, 2007), in protest against the Roman Catholic Church and specific practices such as his protest of indulgences (Wikipedia, 2007), which although Luther was very religious, could not agree with. Luther's contributions included the Lutheran Large Catechism and Small Catechism, and his followers later compiled his thinking into the Book of Concord (Book of Concord, Internet, 2007), which combined the Large and Small Catechisms of Luther, the Apostles' Creed, the Nicene Creed, the Athanasian Creed, the Augsburg Confession, and so on.

[76] Saint Francis Xavier (1506 – 1552 AD) was a Spanish Roman Catholic and co-founder of the Society of Jesus (Wikipedia, 2007).

[77] Alessandro Valignano (1539 – 1606 AD), known to the Chinese as "Fan Li An", was an Italian Jesuit missionary who was known to help Christianity spread to China and Japan (Wikipedia, 2007).

was succeeded by Michele Ruggieri[78] and Matteo Ricci, and Ricci subsequently became one of the best loved and admired Jesuit priests in China, and left many legacies throughout China, even in Hong Kong SAR (Special Administrative Region) and Macau SAR (Gelber, 102). Ricci's success laid with the fact that instead of simply attempting to force the Chinese to be more Western and Christian, he transformed himself to as Chinese as he possibly could, by learning the Chinese culture, even learning the very difficult old form of Chinese language, while teaching the Chinese the more advanced forms of Western mathematics, astronomy, geography, and of course, Christianity.

Learning from Matteo Ricci

Though Christian emissaries are many, the author chose Matteo Ricci as an example of one who was able to maintain his own steadfast Christian contemplation and prayer, while also being able to integrate into an Asian society without prejudice, and with much dedication.

Becoming the Confucian gentleman

Matteo Ricci was born in Italy in 1552 AD, and educated at the Jesuit College of Rome, initially against the wishes of his father. He served in Goa[79] and then Macau[80] in

---

[78] Michele Ruggieri (1543 - 1607 AD) was an Italian Jesuit priest who started missionary work in India and then eventually went to Macau. Like Matteo Ricci, Ruggieri also mastered the old Chinese language (Wikipedia, 2007).

[79] Goa is one of the states in India, situated on the west coast of the nation (Wikipedia, 2007). Goa is described as the smallest state of India in terms of land area.

[80] Macau, now known as Macau Special Administrative Region or SAR, is one of the SARs of China (the other being Hong Kong). The Portuguese ruled it for more than 400 years, and the Portuguese

1582 AD, when he was only thirty years old (Aikman, 45), and learned the rather difficult Chinese language in 1583, and settled in Guangdong province. He only reached Beijing in 1598, and received official sanction to stay in Beijing in 1601, and became one of the rare Christian clergy to receive official stipend[81] until he died in 1610. That bore testimony to Ricci's influence in China (Gelber, 103).

When Ricci started out learning Chinese, he first dressed like a Buddhist monk, as he felt that the Chinese would find it easier to accept him simply as a "Western monk", rather than the still largely unknown Christian priest that he was (Aikman, 45).

Subsequently, Ricci discovered that Buddhist monks were not as respected by the gentry and the officials, just merely accepted and tolerated. He found that the Confucian scholars were much more admired by the masses and especially by the ruling class. Ricci spoke and wrote Chinese, and so he decided to dress like a Chinese Confucian scholar, and ate Chinese food. To the Confucian scholars and Chinese officials who came into contact with Ricci, he was as Chinese and Confucian as anyone of them, and so they accepted him as one of their own (Gelber, 103). This demonstrated that Ricci was highly adaptable and flexible enough to adjust to his surrounding circumstances in order to further God's work in a foreign land.

Another interesting story was that Ricci was a clockmaker, and he presented a Western clock during his first meeting with the Emperor. The Emperor was amused and intrigued by the Western precision clock, and since no

---

influence is still evident in many of the historical buildings as well as the mixed heritage of the residents. It is also one of the most visited tourist locations in Asia (Wikipedia, 2007).

[81] Stipend is an allowance granted by the central government for government officials.

Chinese mechanic knew what to do with the clock, much less adjust it or maintain it, Ricci found a unique small window of opportunity to present Christianity to the Emperor, through a simple clock (Aikman, 45). We find Ricci's work akin to the following, "Take away the wicked from before the king, and his throne shall be established in righteousness. Put not thyself forward in the presence of the king, and stand not in the place of the great" (Proverbs, 25:5-6). We are also reminded to "Show honor to all, love the brotherhood, fear God, love the king" (I Peter, 2:17).

Using secular knowledge to influence the authorities

The Jesuits were renowned for their secular knowledge of sciences, such as complex mathematics, memorization techniques, geography and especially astronomy. Ricci was a humble teacher who imparted all that knowledge to the Chinese. Ricci was said to be able to hear or read a classical Chinese poem just once, and then recite it back effortlessly and properly, which won him many admirers in China, since the Chinese placed great emphasis on knowledge and scholarly pursuits (AIkman, 45).

In ancient times, the Chinese emperor was thought of by the people as a semi-divine entity (called "son of heaven" in Chinese), and one of his primary roles as such an entity, was to determine an accurate calendar that would be adopted nation-wide, so that farmers would be able to harvest well. So a more accurate knowledge of astronomy, as taught by Jesuits such as Ricci, helped to strengthen the support of the Chinese emperor by his people (Gelber, 103). While the Chinese believed their emperor to be semi-divine, the truth is that the emperor and his officials' knowledge of the stars were not quite as profound as they would wish. The Jesuits proved the colossal creation of the one true God through the demonstration of the astronomical knowledge they possess, by simply showing that as emissaries of God, they possessed greater knowledge of the stars compared to the Chinese emperor and his hordes of scholars. The Bible showed the point with the phrase, "And I will give wonders in the heaven above and signs on the earth below, blood, and fire, and vapor of smoke" (Acts, 2:19).

Educating the gentiles on the path of God

Ricci also evangelized Christianity in a subtle and scholarly manner, so that the gentry in China could accept his thoughts without being too defensive or angry. It was well known that the Chinese government at those ancient times was heavily bureaucratic and political, and that one wrong move could easily result in being executed before the public.

Ricci also broke the ice with his Chinese friends, by accepting that Confucianism was not a religion, but rather, just a well-developed ethics system. Ricci also petitioned to Rome that the Chinese form of ancestral rite was merely a civil rite as a sign of respect of elders who passed on, rather than idolatry (Gelber, 104). The Jesuits also managed to get Emperor Kangxi to endorse that such rites were merely civil, not spiritual, affirming the Jesuits' position. This was an important breakthrough in philosophical thought as otherwise, the Chinese would have denounced Christianity, and Christianity would have been lost to other alternative religions.

At the same time, Ricci used Chinese words, rather than Latin words, to allow the Chinese to better understand Christianity. For example, he defined Heaven as "tian", which is the Chinese word for "heaven", and God as "Shang di", which basically means the "Supreme God". By using the local language understood by the Chinese, Ricci was able to evangelize to the Chinese effectively, sharing and using the same language, rather than attempting to get the Chinese to recite Latin prayers that would not make any sense to them (Wright, 114).

Ricci claimed to have baptized one thousand Chinese by 1605 AD. After Ricci's death, more than five thousand Chinese were baptized as Christians (Aikman, 46). Ricci and his successors were able to convert many court eunuchs and women to Christianity, perhaps simply because eunuchs and women were slightly prejudiced against in those times, and Christianity presented itself as a gentle, heartwarming, and touching religion that embraced one and all, and struck an emotional chord with them.

But Ricci was not without detractors, even within his own community in Rome. The Chinese rites were approved by papal Rome in 1615 AD, denounced later in 1645 AD, approved in 1656 AD again, and then denounced by papal Rome once again between 1704 AD and 1715 AD, especially in the issues of Confucianism and ancestral rites. The Chinese was not pleased, and the Emperor literally banned the Christian evangelism and church building by 1717 AD, effectively ending all the good work of Christian evangelism the Jesuits had painstakingly built up, through a wise and conciliatory process of integration and community building (Wright, 115).

Syncretism and guarding against it

Attempting to maintain Christian orthodoxy and yet integrating well into an Asian culture is not without difficulty or challenges. Syncretism has often been said to be the bane of attempting to remain orthodox while integrating into a society that maintains deeply, other faiths or customs.

What syncretism is, or is not

Syncretism is a word derived from the Greek word "synkretismos", which means "a union of communities" (Wikipedia, 2007). Essentially, it usually means a human attempt to reconcile or merge conflicting beliefs or thoughts. The concept is mostly applied when it comes to spirituality, religion and theology.

From the Greek roots, it would appear that syncretism itself might not be wrong, since it is usually an attempt to bring harmony of thoughts together.

Critics on the other hand, tend to use syncretism in a disparaging manner. However, it is relevant to know that if syncretism does not sacrifice the sanctity of the original thought, then it would not blur, dilute, or disturb the true form of the original thought. On the other hand, if syncretism results in confusion, frustration, or even anger, then such a form of syncretism cannot be tolerated. Fundamentally, the Word of God must be theologically interpreted without human bias or prejudice, and if a harmonizing path is chosen to allow gentiles to believe in Christianity, without sacrificing Christian truth, then it can be allowed to happen.

This can be seen in the Jesuits' petition to Rome that the Chinese ancestral rites were merely civil and not spiritual, and therefore not incompatible with Christianity. Opposing factions would dismiss the important and much used civil ancestral rites by the Chinese, rather than finding a way to help the Chinese embrace Christianity and receive Christ's salvation. For example, when people reminisce about their departed relatives, or place bouquets on the graves annually, these are in reality similar to what the Chinese do with their ancestral rites, except perhaps that the Chinese take to a more elaborate visual form. At the heart of both sides, it is nothing more than a civil practice, as a form of reverence to departed and close relatives.

Guarding against syncretism in Asia

While trying to evangelize to pre-believers in Asia, much can be learned from the principles and working approaches of Matteo Ricci, where he did not sacrifice orthodox theology for the sake of trying to win converts.

In today's contemporary world, there seems to be a grave danger for some to "water down", dilute, or over-simply orthodox Christian theology simply to win converts. For example, it is less often that ministers discuss or evangelize the difficult path of Christian discipleship, such as the exalted approach of the Beatitudes[82], which can be a tall order for any Christian to attempt and attain. However, as servants of the Word, it is important to remember that we should strive to win true disciples for God, and not simply to fill up "slots" in the church, or simply attempting to build large numbers or empires for vanity (Prime, Begg, 2004, 49).

Finding common ground with an ecumenical heart

The indigenous cultures in Asia have their proud lineage and history, and we should attempt to respect their background, while gently introducing the Christian faith. Often, cultural diversity requires cultural sensitivity, diplomacy, compassion, humility and gentility.

---

[82] The most defining work on not only attaining moral authority, but also more than that, to attain holiness and true happiness, was the Beatitudes (which in Latin "beatitudo" means happiness). In the Beatitudes (Matthew, 5:3-12), Jesus described the qualities for the citizens of the Kingdom of heaven, and explained what it meant to be truly blessed and enjoy fellowship with God.

For example, in Asian locations such as Thailand, it would be difficult to find a local resident negating our comments openly or confronting us blatantly. Likewise, in locations such as Japan, where courtesy is sometimes very extensive and developed, the residents may never openly deny our ideas or suggestions, but would suggest that they would convene in a committee meeting and revert back to us. Invariably, they may never return to communicate with us again. Therefore, confrontational and direct approaches often would fail in many parts of Asia, especially when we are discussing something as deep and innately important as religion.

For successful ministering and evangelism, it might be important to adopt a mindset of finding similarities, rather than intentionally uncovering differences, between Christian and various Asian practices.

For example, renowned Trappist[83] monk, mystic and writer, Thomas Merton[84], was known for his ecumenical heart when facing other faiths. He remained a strict Christian monk, and at no time did his orthodoxy, contemplation and prayer faltered. He was widely regarded as a theologian and contemplative thinker, even by those of other faiths, including His Holiness (HH) the Dalai Lama[85].

---

[83] Trappists are monks belonging to the Order of Cistercians of the Strict Observance (O.C.S.O.), or Ordo Cisterciensis Strictioris Observantiae, a Roman Catholic religious order that follows the Rule of Saint Benedict (Wikipedia, 2007).
[84] Thomas Merton (1915 - 1968 AD) belongs to the Trappist monastic order, at the Abbey of Our Lady of Gethsemani, in Kentucky, USA. He is one of the established Catholic authors in the 20th century, with over 60 published books (Wikipedia, 2007).
[85] The Dalai Lama actually refers to a religious lineage of monks in Tibet that are under the Gelugpa sect of Tibetan Buddhism. The Dalai Lama is also the temporal titleholder of Tibet in ancient times. However, when we discuss the Dalai Lama in the modern day context, we usually refer to

From Merton's approach in our contemporary world, we find that Merton not only shows a true ecumenical and compassionate heart when attempting to reach out to pre-believers, he is in fact very similar to his much more ancient brethren Jesuit priest Matteo Ricci. For example, both Merton and Ricci learned the scriptures and works of the pre-believers, before attempting to converse, communicate, and share the Gospel with them. Merton read complex Zen scriptures of Buddhism, by Shantideva[86] and many others, before he communicated his Christian thoughts and beliefs to accomplished Buddhist practitioners such as HH Dalai Lama. Likewise, Ricci also learned the Confucian Analects, even mastered the ancient Chinese language (something very difficult even for the contemporary Chinese themselves), before he ministered and preached to the Chinese pre-believers in the Ming Dynasty. The author believes that for effective evangelism to Asian pre-believers to materialize, some degree of dedicated study, or at least cursory understanding in a holistic context of different faiths, is important. At the same time, after researching seriously into such works, it would serve to reinforce the minister's own Christian beliefs and his faith in God, to be able to share the Gospel even more convincingly.

Common ground and orthodoxy

There are many indigenous faiths in Asia, including Buddhism, Taoism, Confucianism, Hinduism, and Islam. For the purpose of discussion, the author will focus on

---

the 14th Dalai Lama who has the name of Tenzin Gyatso (Wikipedia, 2007).

[86] Shantideva was an 8th century Indian Buddhist scholar, noted for his work "Bodhicaryavatara" ("Guide to the Bodhisattva's Way of Life"), essentially an instruction manual for anyone who wishes to practice the path of compassion for the sake of others (Wikipedia, 2007).

faiths such as Buddhism, Taoism, and Confucianism, which are prevalent in ancient China to today.

Within Buddhism, there are three primary vehicles or paths, known as Vajrayana[87], Mahayana[88], and Theravada[89]. There are three forms of Taoism, Philosophical Taoism (Zhuangzi's[90] "Nanhua Zhenjing", or "True Scripture of the Southern Florescence"), Religious Taoism (Lao Zi's[91] "Dao De Jing" or "Scripture of the way and ethics"), and Folk Taoism. Confucianism is less of a religion but more of an operating philosophy, developed and written by Chinese scholar Confucius[92]. Hinduism is polytheistic and has many deities, each serving a primary function for its believers.

---

[87] Vajrayana ("vajra" is diamond, and "yana" is vehicle) is one of the main branches of Buddhism, whereby skilled teachers teach esoteric or Tantric meditative methods, and students must receive an initiation for each practice method. Vajrayana is primarily rooted in Tibet, Nepal, and pockets within India (Wikipedia, 2007).

[88] Mahayana ("maha" is greater) stresses on exercising compassion and sacrifice on behalf of others, and practitioners seek perfection for others before oneself. Mahayana is primarily rooted in China, Taiwan, Hong Kong SAR, and Japan (Wikipedia, 2007).

[89] Theravada ("the way of the elders") is also known as Hinayana ("Hina" is smaller), seeks enlightenment through contemplation and advice from the elders, and the ultimate goal is to reach the stage of Arhat (Sanskrit for "the worthy one"). Theravada is primarily practiced in Sri Lanka, and many parts of Indo-China, including Thailand, Laos, Cambodia and Myanmar (Wikipedia, 2007).

[90] Zhuangzi was a 4th century BCE Chinese philosopher during the Warring States period. His philosophy showed a lamentation of the limits of humans and the infinite unlimited universe. In this regard, it can be observed that his works demonstrated a parallel to the Christian understanding of the smallness and limitations of man versus the infinite nature and manifestation of God (Wikipedia, 2007).

[91] Lao Zi was a 6th century BCE Chinese philosopher who was attributed as the author of Dao De Jing, a literature that described the Taoist path and ethics.

[92] Confucius (551 - 479 BCE) was a Chinese philosopher who wrote the Analects, which stressed contemplative study over elaborate rituals, and

Buddhism, at a greater level, is also more of an operating philosophy geared at wisdom development, and does not really share the complex deistic nature of say, Folk Taoism and Hinduism. The Buddhas (fully awakened beings), Bodhisattvas (great compassionate beings), and Arhats (lesser awakened beings), are more like sages and saints. Although folk practices among the older generation in Asia seem to pervade the misunderstanding among Christians that Buddhists "pray" to these Buddhas, Bodhisattvas and Arhats, the reality is that the more learned ones who studied and contemplated on the Buddhist scriptures understand that reverence to these beings is the key, not prayer. Therefore, in order for a Christian minister to evangelize to Buddhists, the right understanding and much reading is required. Otherwise, all too frequently, preachers without any understanding into Buddhism, will get shut out very quickly since the initial contact would already show the Buddhist pre-believers that the preachers have no understanding of their faiths.

One of the common concepts in Asian religions such as Buddhism and Hinduism is the concept of "karma", or cause and effect. For example, if a person murders another, the heavy sin of murder will have a repercussion on this person, whereby it is likely that he would receive an equivalent punishment of death somehow, perhaps by the family of the person he killed, or by others, including that of the state government.

Therefore, in the Asian religious context, the "cause" is this person murdering another, and the "effect" will be his punishment of death later on. "Karma" therefore can be seen as a causal loop of events. This concept of "karma" is

---

his works are still used in many parts of Asia today, together with translated thoughts throughout contemporary Western practices (Wikipedia, 2007).

not difficult to explain in the Christian context, when preaching to pre-believers of other faiths in Asia.

It is said in the Bible, "For each shall bear his own burden. Let him that is taught in the word communicate to him that teaches in all good things. Be not deceived: God is not mocked; for whatever a man shall sow, that also shall he reap. For he that sows to his own flesh, shall reap corruption from the flesh; but he that sows to the Spirit, from the Spirit shall reap eternal life: but let us not lose heart in doing good; for in due time, if we do not faint, we shall reap" (Galatians, 6:5-9).

Therefore, there is a causal loop of events, when a person commits crimes and sins against others, and that he would have to bear his own burden of these crimes and sins. It is also stated clearly in the Galatians, that "God is not mocked; for whatever a man shall sow, that also shall he reap". If we can show this passage to a pre-believer who believes strongly in the concept of "karma", it is entirely possible that this pre-believer will be able to find acceptance and convergence of the concepts.

In the Christian commandments, we also see a lot of convergence in the ethics and morality shared by other faiths, which will allow Christian ministers to share with pre-believers of other faiths. For example, "Honor thy Mother and Father" ranks very highly in Asian cultures. It is very common for Asian children to remain in the same residence with their parents even after they have matured into their forties, or are married, while Western counterparts would have moved out of parental homes in adulthood. The civil rites of ancestral reverence are also an expression of honoring parents and older generations. The rest of the Christian commandments of not committing murder, adultery, theft, false witness, lust, and greed, are all common moral values Asians treasure, whether it be Confucian ethics, or any one of the other Asian faiths.

For this discussion, the author shall not discuss Folk and Religious Taoism, but use only the Philosophical Taoism as a point of reference and comparison. The Beatitudes also showed the way of a Christian disciple, many moral qualities that can be found in Taoism's Three Treasures ("san bao"), which are compassion ("ci"), moderation ("jian" or economy) and humility.

Confucianism's[93] common concepts frequently taught to young children in parts of Asia include filial piety ("xiao"), humaneness ("ren"), and being a gentleman ("junzi"). Therefore, Confucianism is not a religion, but rather, a philosophical and ethics system.

Buddhism is also a very developed philosophy that started in India and permeates many other parts of Indo-China, North Asia, and some pockets of South East Asia.

One of Tibet's exalted contemplative teachers, Milarepa[94], can be used as an analogy to sinners who can receive redemption. Although obviously nothing similar theologically to Christianity, when faced with the need to discuss the concept of human sinners who can receive redemption, the story of Milarepa will be useful to bridge a gap, when discussing the redemptive power of Christ even if one is soaked in grave sin. This can possibly gain favor with pre-believers who are aware of personal sins and trespasses, and are actively seeking a path of redemption. After all, not everyone, especially contemporary people, will be willing or

---

[93] Confucianism is literally translated as the path of the scholars, and is defined as an ethical and philosophical secular system developed by early Chinese sage Confucius (Wikipedia, 2007).

[94] Milarepa (1052 – 1135 CE) is one of Tibet's well-known early Buddhist teachers (Wikipedia, 2007).

able to subject themselves to the grueling redemptive regime Milarepa went through. However, the redemption of Christ is inclusive, complete, healing, and much more achievable when compared to the path Milarepa had to take.

Milarepa murdered 35 people when close relatives robbed his immediate family and its wealth, but through a punishing physical and spiritual purgatory by his spiritual teacher Marpa, he was able to purge his sins and eventually reached his enlightenment. A minister can use the Milarepa example to show how the loving God also draws a parallel, whereby God's salvation is for all humans who are sinners, who can receive His grace and redemption, through accepting Jesus Christ, and thereafter, walking a holy path in imitation of Christ.

Another common Chinese story that finds parallel with God's saving grace for us is related to the Zen Buddhist phrase, "Leave the butcher's knife behind and become enlightened". The fable was of a monk named "Runge" (Dizang.org, Internet, 2007). Before he became a monk, he was a butcher and killed sheep for profit. As Runge was about to slaughter a goat, the goat screamed for dear life. Coincidentally, the Buddhist Fifth Patriarch strolled by and pacified the goat. Runge was curious why the goat stopped screaming, and asked the Fifth Patriarch. The Patriarch replied, "Your past life was a goat and the goat you are about to kill was a butcher. He killed you then. Now you are about to kill the goat as a butcher. In the future, the goat will return as a butcher and kill you then, when you will return as a goat. This endless loop will go on." Runge heard it, broke down into tears and knelt down in repentance, and let the goat go. Runge eventually became a contemplative monk who reached great spiritual awareness.

Using tiered strategy of W.E.B.

The author uses the acronym of W.E.B. to describe the ideological starting points when ministering to various communities in Asia. The acronym W.E.B. stands for Works, Evangelism, and Brotherhood.

Each of these pathways and methods are used for distinct community groups, which the author humbly believes is more efficient and effective when attempting to minister to these different groups, since each of these groups will have different demands out of life, and also require different emotive and physical approaches.

Works - Humanitarian works, funding and helping

One area which pastors can demonstrate and convince the needy, is not just through evangelism, but more so, through works. It was said, "Let your light thus shine before men, so that they may see your upright works, and glorify your Father who is in the heavens" (Matthew, 5:16).

Some detractors may believe that if Christians provided humanitarian aid to less privileged communities, there is no physical difference from other groups giving the same aid.

However, Wiersbe asserted that the biggest difference between Christian ministry and mere humanitarian benevolence is that only Christian ministry can put grace in the heart so that lives can be changed and problems are solved intrinsically (Wiersbe, 1993, 21). Therefore, as Christian ministers and communities provide aid to others, they are bestowed a unique opportunity to allow others to see the light they provide as Christians, and invariably, be drawn to them to listen to the Word of God. We are reminded of what Jesus said, "Ye are the light of the world" (Matthew, 5:14). As Christians, it is our duty to give and provide in honor and glory of God, for the benefit of others. Further, Wiersbe said, "Ministry takes place when divine resources meet human needs through loving channels to the glory of God" (Wiersbe, 14), which means that our ministry when we are fulfilling human needs, must be done with love, and for the glory of God only.

Bi-vocational pastors, such as the author, can perhaps lend a financial hand at very needy communities, whether it is through the building of basic infrastructure, the provision of basic living necessities, or the building of secular educational systems and framework. Pastors, whether bi-vocational or full-time, can certainly also provide pastoral care through counseling, chaplaincy, and sometimes just simply being a compassionate and patient listener.

At the same time, pastors can reach out to the needy by engaging and rallying able-bodied and financially endowed community members to extend a helping hand to the needy communities, acting as peacemaker and facilitator. This was said as, "... for the perfecting of the saints, with a view to the work of the ministry, with a view to the edifying of the body of Christ" (Ephesians, 4:12). One such group is the Servants to Asia's Urban Poor (Wikipedia, 2007), which helps the underprivileged in some of the most impoverished parts of Asia, through humanitarian works with a Christian focus.

Humanitarian or mission works are expressions of showing the compassion and love of Christ to others, such as said, "thou shalt love thy neighbor as thyself" (Mark, 12:31). Therefore, pastors can take lead to encourage believers to show compassion and love to others in need, all God's children, through humanitarian works. Such works must be done in the context of glorifying the unconditional and unending love of Christ, and not for self or corporate glorification. There should not be the thought of seeking rewards, returns, or praise, but rather, simply as an expression of our walking in imitation of Christ.

Evangelism - To the spiritually seeking

The charisma or God's gift of pastors and teachers cannot be taken lightly, especially in the context of the priesthood of all believers. There is a divine reason God has empowered pastors and teachers with the ability and the willingness to teach, as mentioned in the Bible, "...and He has given some apostles, and some prophets, and some evangelists, and some shepherds and teachers," (Ephesians, 4:11). This means that some are chosen by God to be ordained to the task of teaching and evangelizing, and God does have specific plans for everyone, as are the mysteries of faith as a collective body of Christ (Prime, Begg, 14, 58).

There is a distinction between teaching and preaching (Prime, Begg, 125). As teachers, we seek to educate people to understand God's truth. As preachers, we hope to tug at their wills and hearts, by making an emotional and passionate appeal, however subtle, so that they can take another step forward with action, rather than simply understanding God's truth.

It is insufficient to preach only the niceties and pleasantries that the Gospel, being the "Good News", contains.

There are also many grave and serious, and very enlightening passages in the Bible that preachers must endorse, affirm, evangelize, and repeat. As the Chinese saying goes, "good medicine always tastes bitter". For example, Scottish missionary William Chalmers Burns[95]

---

[95] William Chalmers Burns, a Christian evangelist, was also like Matteo Ricci, who wore Chinese clothes while evangelizing in China, for twenty

said, "How hard it is to unite in just proportions the humbling doctrine of man's inability to come to Christ without regeneration, and the free gospel offer which is the moral means employed by God in conversion! Oh! Spirit of Jesus, my Savior, lead me, a poor, ignorant, and self-conceited sinner, to the experience of this great mystery of grace, that I may know how I ought to declare thy glorious gospel to perishing fellow-sinners! Amen" (Prime, Begg, 53).

One of the hallmarks of the Bible is that it is inspiring (Erickson, 2006, 226). While the Bible tells of historical instances, analogies and parables in rather poetic ways, as well as having terrifying stories of punitive measures against sin, the underlying message is often one that urges us on with inspiration, and empowers us to be able to stride forward with greater confidence and strength. Inspiration in the Bible takes two paths, one of supernatural occurrences, and one of ordinary but entirely moving emotive events. Therefore, while we think of many of the strategic pitches and tactical methods, we must also harness the entirety of the inspiring and emotive parts of the Bible, which often touches the heart much deeper, and would allow us to get closer to the pre-believer.

Brotherhood - Bonding with the accomplished

There are many fraternities or community-based organizations that do many good humanitarian works in aid of other communities or groups in need, especially in Asia.

For example, the Rotary movement[96] is very established in many South East Asia locations, including Singapore,

---

years, before dying from an illness at Niu Zhuang, near Beijing, in 1868 AD (Wikipedia, 2007).

[96] The Rotary International movement (rotary.org), founded by Paul Harris, is an umbrella organization with more than 32,000 independent clubs and more than 1.2 million members around the world, under the

Malaysia, and Taiwan. The Rotary clubs are independently managed by a small group of volunteers, typically successful and accomplished people in business, professions, and academia. Each Rotary club is around forty people, and they would generally meet regularly at least once a week, to update each other on the progress of humanitarian work on the ground. The individual Rotary Clubs then come under a regional management known as a District, with a volunteer Governor and a board to manage regional activities. Collectively, such volunteer fraternity or community organizations have helped many others, from as little as providing meals to the poor aged, vaccination for the under-developed regions in other countries, to re-building homes and schools for disaster-struck areas.

In the light of such community organizations run completely by volunteers, we can find a way to engage such organizations and their members, to find some synergy with Christianity. For pre-believers who are actively seeking a deeper meaning to life and thinking that Christianity is the key, personalized evangelism with individual members of such fraternities and community organizations would be likely to be met with less resistance.

The author can point to a personal example when he was the community service director for a local Rotary club, of a Christian Rotarian who works in the civil service, and yet find time to volunteer at the Prisons, to minister to the in-mates, especially for those who would like to seek spiritual solace and refuge in Christ. And because of his

---

same visual and operating identity. Members are known as Rotarians. The organization seeks to provide humanitarian help around the world. One of its more illustrious works is PolioPlus, which is an ambitious global project aimed at eradicating the debilitating disease of polio in the entire world. Under PolioPlus, Rotarians provide free vaccination for children in underdeveloped nations, through financial aid and volunteering in the field (Wikipedia, 2007).

ministering to the social causes, his fellow Rotarians look to him as a guiding light, and are more sympathetic to listen to him.

Problem-solving during evangelism

There are many ways to evangelize to pre-believers, as well as believers in various stages of their Christian discipleship.

The author humbly suggests some process methods derived from his corporate consulting work, which can be equally applied in the complex and difficult path of chaplaincy and ministering.

Evangelizing process - groups or individual

The process of evangelizing cannot be a mechanistic process, since it involves human beings with complex intellectual and emotional nuances, especially pre-believers, with their own preset beliefs (or non-beliefs), backgrounds, cultural and linguistic differences, emotions, and personalities.

Therefore, the author's suggestions in the evangelistic process when in Asia would at best be recommendations, given the unique field with highly diverse cultures and practices that would deviate from the standard norms when compared to evangelizing in the Western developed nations.

At the same time, even if the evangelist is well prepared and equipped with orthodox Christian knowledge of the Bible and commentaries, it is still insufficient. Preparation must be done before attempting to approach pre-believers. The author suggests the following process of steps that mirrors a typical corporate pitch process.

One of the common failings of an evangelist in Asia is the use of "hell and brimstone" approach, which has been often used by some minorities, and yet consistently resisted by pre-believers. An extension of the "hell and brimstone" approach is to attempt to trap or corner the pre-believers with ideology, arguments, or statements which are unknown or not yet proven to the pre-believers. Again, since most people resist change, and that most people do not take well to things forced unto them, the aggressive method must therefore be avoided in Asia.

The author has previously authored a corporate training program aimed at major account servicing using a process approach H.O.P.E., which stands for Historical, Obstacle, Projection, and End-results. The same process can be applied during Christian evangelism.

Historical - fact-finding and investigating

Before evangelizing to an individual or groups of pre-believers, the evangelist may want to find out as much as possible the backgrounds, preferences, cultures, and any other attributes or characteristics which would help the evangelist in reaching out to the pre-believers more effectively. It is unwise, and even arrogant, to simply approach pre-believers and immediately teach or speak of the Gospel, since there would invariably be large chasms of understanding to cross, and great theological and fundamental philosophical divides to conquer.

Also, in the context of a large group, just a few dissenting and loud pre-believers may negate the evangelist's best efforts to reach out to the rest of the large group. It might even be wise to break down larger groups into smaller groups, or even evangelize to individuals instead. The minister may need to assess the situation with God's guidance, to discern how small a group should be, or even down to individual evangelism.

To use the analogy of the corporate world, a typical insurance agent would likely approach family members first, then friends, and then make cold calls to solicit complete strangers, when attempting to sell insurance policies. This is simply because generally people would know family members very well, including their idiosyncrasies. Friends are also easier to approach, and complete strangers would present much greater challenges since the insurance agent do not know anything about the person and needs.

So in the context of evangelism, the evangelist can attempt to find out about an individual pre-believer's preference for food, leisure, literature, and belief systems. The approach required by an evangelist when approaching an atheist is different from that of a pantheist or a polytheist. There is no simple "umbrella" approach when attempting to evangelize to a group of pre-believers. Each person brings unique requests, demands, and spiritual needs to the table.

Once the parameters of the personality and beliefs of the pre-believer are established as much as possible, the evangelist can then strategize how best to present the Gospel to the pre-believer. The evangelist can also begin to identify quotes and particular passages from the Bible, and start to formulate a general outline of the conversation that will take place. It may seem tedious, but preparation is key to evangelism, especially to Asians with deep conviction and beliefs. The evangelist may then run through the presentation format and substance, either alone, or with a group of like-minded evangelists, before meeting with the pre-believer at the agreed upon location for the meeting.

Obstacle - Explore questions, doubts, and concerns.

When ministering to pre-believers, we must recognize the uphill obstacles we will face when attempting to convert them to Christianity.

To reduce objections to mundane issues outside of Christianity, ministering to a single pre-believer is best achieved in social and casual settings, which would put both the minister and the pre-believer at ease. Conversely, for a large group of pre-believers, the author believes that using open, honest facilitation works best. Facilitating a Christian discussion with a larger group of skeptical pre-believers is quite akin to facilitating a discussion with a group of company chief executives. One of the common methods of facilitation is known as Open Space Technology (OST)[97], made popular by Harrison Owen. OST is often used by corporate executives confronted with major challenges, and any stakeholder can step into the OST session to present possible solutions to the problems, and the session continues until the problem is solved, or action steps recorded down properly to facilitate future action to work towards a resolution of the problem.

At the actual meeting, the evangelist can then choose a mutually agreeable location to meet the pre-believer, and attempt to make the experience as pleasant as possible for the pre-believer. The evangelist can identify the preferred

---

[97] Open Space Technology (OST) is a method for facilitating meetings aimed at solving problems with a group of people. It is made popular by Harrison Owen since 1986, inspired by ancient Native American traditions of groups of people sitting around an open space to resolve issues and challenges together. OST is different from normal meetings which are led or controlled by a leader or facilitator where every participant has to comply with the leader's guidance or restrictions. OST allows more open collaboration, with no personal agenda, to simply attempt to solve often difficult problems (Wikipedia, Internet, 2007).

location to evangelize, based on the pre-believer's personality and personal preferences. For example, some people may prefer spicy food, while others may prefer lighter cuisine. The choice of the location should not be too ostentatious, nor should it be too noisy and dirty to be distracting to both the minister and the pre-believer. The food served at the location should not distract the pre-believer to only focus on how good the food is, and neither should be the food served be so unpalatable that the pre-believer yearns to leave the table early. In many parts of South East Asia, the relative humidity may reach as high as 90 percent, with very high temperatures sometimes approaching over thirty-five degrees Celsius (around 95 degrees Fahrenheit). Therefore, it is very difficult for a pre-believer to listen to the minister in relative comfort in open-air environments in many parts of South East Asia. An air-conditioned environment may be entirely necessary.

According to theologian Willard, God's kingdom permeates throughout all existence, and it is not an external, remote location, that we aspire to, said by Jesus Christ, "Thy kingdom come, on earth as it is in heaven" (Willard, 1997, 26). However, even as God's universal love and compassion is meant for all, not everyone is ready and willing to accept and surrender to His will. Many times, pre-believers, and even Christians, do not surrender to God's will to allow God's kingdom to become evident in our lives.

Therefore, as a minister with a genuine conviction to help pre-believers embrace Christianity, we must recognize that sometimes some pre-believers whose lives we come into contact with, may never embrace Christianity. Some other pre-believers whom we may come into contact with, may not convert to Christianity under our care, but with God's will, will be convinced at some farther point in time.

Willard eloquently explained that God is inherently holy and loving, that is His intrinsic nature. Therefore, the entire universe being His creation, He has utmost tender love and fondness for all of it, including us (Willard, 62). Therefore, God can only love us with genuine liking and fondness, and not like the shallow tolerance that human love for each other is. The Bible specifically mentioned that God said, "Call unto me, and I will answer thee, and I will show thee great and hidden things, which thou knowest not" (Jeremiah, 33:3). This is yet another example that God does not neglect or leave any of His children behind, as He truly shows His infinite love, compassion, and gracious salvation for one and all. This is a compelling point to always be brought forth to pre-believers, as it removes many of the mental doubts and barriers from them.

Willard mentioned something rather dramatic and compelling, by asserting that Jesus and God hear anyone who calls upon Them, and not just listen to the baptized believers (Willard, 32). This is compelling and powerful as it means that for evangelists attempting to reach out to pre-believers with an interest or curiosity to want to learn about Christianity, this is a persuasive comment, rather different from the segregationist approach of "they versus us". Willard explains that since all of us, being God's creations, live in His ecos (Hebrews, 3:4). Therefore, Willard asserted that since we live in God's universe, God cannot but hear us whenever and whoever calls His name. God's love is all encompassing and overarching, waiting patiently and kindly for us to lean on Him, to receive the salvation He so graciously gives to us. Pre-believers will begin to recognize the immense grace God bestows upon His children, and will slowly be attracted and drawn towards such a magnanimous ideology eventually.

When God created humankind, He made no distinction to ethnicity, gender, or economic status

(Erickson, 558). The diversity was embraced by God as all of His creation, and the prejudices are all humans' own creation. Also, one must not neglect or disrespect the aged, for God's Bible also valued the aged (Erickson, 568). For example, ancient Hebrews and the Orientals (the Chinese) held the aged in utmost respect, as the aged demonstrated learned wisdom and deep experience in life (Erickson, 569). Therefore, for prejudiced segments of the communities the minister attempts to evangelize to, God's all encompassing love for all of His creation can be emphasized and explained further to the pre-believers. Often, disenfranchised segments of communities, such as the aged or the prejudiced gender, would find emotive and spiritual resonance with the Gospel.

Willard warns of being just a "bumper sticker" Christian (Willard, 1997, 41), since some may mistakenly believe that salvation is simply bestowed and that one can continue on his merry and wicked ways. When ministering to pre-believers, we must not over-simplify Christianity to simply hope to convert them without bringing them into the full fold as Christian disciples on a lifelong pursuit of a life in imitation of Christ. Willard quoted Anglican Bishop Stephen Neill, "To be a Christian means to be like Jesus Christ" (Willard, 42), a tall and demanding order no less, but one that reminds us of the colossal challenges we face as Christians, and that God's path is intended for the courageous, not the complacent. Even if obstacles abound when we minister to pre-believers, we must not dilute the message of the Gospel, and should faithfully and dutifully also explain the tougher parts of Christianity, knowing that it may present a steeper challenge for us as ministers. We must trust in God that the full splendor of God's truth will eventually prevail, whether through our humble laboring hands and tongues, or through others, or even through some wondrous manifestation of God's grace on the pre-believer's life at some point in time.

One of the dangers of trying to preach to pre-believers is to remove the deity of Christ (Willard, 56). Willard believes that some modernists tend to remove the deity of Christ to reduce Christ to simply being a great teacher. Some preachers may attempt to do this in the hope that pre-believers, especially those who cannot see supernatural manifestations as possible or real, may find it more palatable to accept a human Christ, rather than Christ the Son of God. But the danger is that one this road is taken, the pre-believer will split the Bible apart, and reduce all supernatural manifestations as unimportant or worse, untrue, thereby removing the inerrancy of God's Word, and not being able to accept the full mysteries of faith.

The Bible clearly said, "But I say to all of you: In the future you will see the Son of Man sitting at the right hand of the Mighty One and coming on the clouds of heaven" (Matthew, 26: 63). Why is the deity of Christ important? The deity of Christ implies that we can gain real knowledge of God, since Jesus taught us many things about God. The deity of Christ also brings real redemption, as He sacrificed His life for us. The deity of Christ also brings communion once again, between God and man, exalted through prayer (Erickson, 2006, 720). But at the same time, the humanity of Christ (Erickson, 721) must not be diminished or negated, even as the concept of Christ as a human being is not as hotly debated as the deity of Christ. And though Christ was definitely human, He differed from us with His holiness and sinless nature (Erickson, 735), and therefore, as a human being united with God (Erickson, 749), He could redeem us by offering Himself as the ultimate sacrifice.

One of the frequently asked questions by pre-believers is why there are so much schism within the Christian faith, with numerous denominations that do not seem to see eye to eye. For a minister to be successful with the conversion of doubtful pre-believers, he may need to remember that at the end of the day, it is God's kingdom he is helping to build, humbly as a simple servant and laborer of the Word, nothing more. While we sometimes see errant ministers going about expanding their own personal territories and failing to put God first, as defenders and advocates of the faith, we must not succumb to such errancy. Therefore, when pre-believers ask of us, it would be wise to be open to the pre-believers that God's kingdom is indeed vast and sometimes beyond our limited human comprehension. It is the duty of a minister to allow the pre-believer to have the freedom to choose, not only whether or not the pre-believer would embrace Christianity, but also the freedom to choose whichever mainstream denomination that best appeal to the pre-believer. For example, there are Christians who would prefer a sober communion and prayer, while there are others who much prefer a highly energized, musically charged, and passionate sermon. A minister can only guide the pre-believer to as orthodox a path as humanly possible, and leave it to God's time and will, such that the Holy Spirit will bring orthodoxy, faith, and righteousness, into the new believer's lifetime. Christian writer Osbeck quoted an unknown source in his works; "A Christian is a person who, when getting to the end of his/her rope, ties a knot and determines to hang on, realizing that human extremity now becomes God's opportunity" (Osbeck, 2002, 291). Therefore, it is wise to remember that God will always have the right answer, at the right time, at the right place, and that as mere channels for His work, we can simply trust that He will make His will be done.

One of the frequently raised objections to the presence of God in the Christian context is the topic of evil and sin. There is moral evil, which is driven by humans themselves, against other humans. Erickson explained that God certainly did not create sin, but merely provided the means and options available for human free will. Therefore, only humans and the fallen angels have sinned, not God (Erickson, 454). At the same time, we must not think that suffering or calamity we experience is a direct translation or manifestation of some specific sin. For example, if we are born blind, it does not necessarily imply we committed a particular sin to be born blind (Erickson, 454). God is deeply grieved by humans sinning against Him, as said in Genesis 6:6, much as a loving father would be deeply grieved when a child turns into a criminal and is ultimately jailed for his crimes. On the issue of hell, it is the same as a human's choice of turning to sin. Some people would consistently turn God away throughout life, telling God to "go away" or "leave me alone". Therefore, due to the cumulative mental state of such people, ultimately God grants the wishes of such people, which is the state of hell itself.

Projection – Witnessing and anticipating results

The Christian minister, having established the history through investigation and preparation, and having overcome obstacles during theological discussion, can now be a witness for Christ, in this step of "projection".

Once the environment has settled the pre-believer in comfort, the evangelist can then witness for Christ and evangelize the Gospel, within the refined framework he or she has prepared beforehand. The pre-believer can be allowed, and in fact should be encouraged to ask questions, and the evangelist should be open-minded to allow all manners of questions. Since it is impossible for the evangelist to provide all answers, the evangelist can show sincerity and earnestness by writing down all unanswered questions, and then asking the pre-believer to give time so that the evangelist can find out from other learned sources later on. It is also important to give a specified date and place for another meeting, whereby the evangelist can provide the answers to these unanswered questions later on at a promised date and time.

In the case of witnessing, there may be a broad spectrum of very personal and yet profound occurrences that the evangelist personally experienced, which would demonstrate the Living Christ and the Holy Spirit in action. However, care must be taken to do this with the greatest of sensibility and sensitivity to the pre-believer. For example, to an atheist, the approach would need to be different from evangelizing to pantheists or polytheists. To an atheist, perhaps it may be wise, at least initially, to reduce the mention of supernatural events such as healing, and instead focus more on the moral and ethical side of the Bible, and how that works in tandem with recognized humanistic values. For pre-believers who believe in the supernatural, then it is likely to present more supernatural miracles God has blessed the minister, or people the minister has helped or got to know in his life.

"Blessed they who have not seen and have believed," Jesus said to Thomas (John 20:29). We must not create segregation in believers, where there are some who receive God's spiritual signs and messages, and those who do not. There is no "elite" believer, as all are God's children, equal in sin and in salvation.

The pre-believers would often ask just how a Christian journey would be like. God's grace provides the means to salvation, but first, we get a calling from God. He does that through various ways. When someone comes into contact with the Bible, that is God's calling to allow us to study the Gospel and when we encounter a phrase such as when Jesus said, "Come to me, all you who are wear and burdened, and I will give you rest" (Matthew, 11:28), many of us would be moved and will let go of our doubts and fears, and turn to

God. God also works through the Holy Spirit to bring extraordinary personal experiences to pre-believers, and allow them to see the truth and grace of God, and in so, turn towards God. Next, we convert to the Christian way of life, and walk ever forward in a long, arduous process of sanctification (Erickson, 946). Along the way, we falter and fall, frequently, and we must repent for our sins and pray for God's forgiveness (Erickson, 947). And as we study, pray, and contemplate, we build on our faith in God, by allowing God to worry for the mundane things, as we trust God ever more and more (Erickson, 951). God will also regenerate us, by renewing us through a supernatural process of "new birth" (Erickson, 958). As Christians, God does not simply leave us alone to try to scale the mountains to reach Him. Rather, He continuously helps the transformative process to allow us to be sanctified in the image of Christ, as we lean and move forward to Him (Erickson, 979). God will also exercise His irresistible grace continuously so that we can remain in our faith in Him. Despair and desperation will attempt to falter us now and then, but God will ease away the despairs through His miraculous and sometimes subtle works, so that we as believers can remain faithful (Erickson, 996), and ultimately, allow us to be glorified in His name. It is not sheer optimism and hope that God gives, but the fact that in Christ's second coming, we will be perfect and complete (Erickson, 1013). One can receive this salvation through the means of receiving, reading, contemplating, and praying through the Word of God (Erickson, 1021).

End-results of successful conversion, or open dialog

To persuade a pre-believer to accept Christ as Savior will usually take more than a single session. The minister needs to be patient and resolute in wanting to bring a pre-believer to God, while remaining gentle, open, and communicative in demeanor at all time. It is much easier to bring a pre-believer to God if the pre-believer trusts and likes the minister as a friend. At the same time, perhaps it would be wise for the minister to focus less on a finite end-result and time frame that he desires, but rather, allow God's infinite grace to get the job done, at His time. A minister should preferably seek to form meaningful relationships with the pre-believer, which inherently works better at conversion than simply aggressively trying to convert Asians.

To a polytheist, it is also important to not get into a heated argument immediately on ideology such as that of one God versus many gods. Rather, the minister can simply focus on the teachings of Christ to his apostles and believers, without focusing too strongly, at least initially, on the concept of one God. Gently coax the pre-believer, without undue pressure, by listening more, talking of parables and stories told within the Bible, and very gently converging towards the passages that can raise arguments eventually. An evangelist shares the parallel with a professional salesperson or a consultant, in that both persons must take a gentle, cooperative, and empathetic approach when trying to persuade someone to accept a view or product.

Styles of influencing

To influence someone is a process of negotiation, or better yet, persuasion. The Latin definition of negotiation is also interesting, stating that "neg" (not) and "otium" (leisure), which means that negotiation is a conspicuous process that is not easy.

Negotiation has many interpretations. For example, it is a process of influencing another's behavior. It is also a process of changing a relationship, hopefully for the better. To the extreme, it can be a process where parties with conflicting goals establish the terms of which they will cooperate, with a firm action to be achieved. Negotiation is rarely a one-step or one-off event. It is split into pre-negotiation, formal negotiation, and post-negotiation. It can even be looping, where you go back to either pre-negotiation or formal negotiation, in the event that things are not agreeable. Just as a family or marital relationship, negotiation is an on-going relationship that requires continued feeding, nurturing, and refinement.

Unlike negotiation, persuasion seeks to move the other party to adopt one's own beliefs. Negotiation however, is the meeting at a compromised mid-point. Winston Churchill once chatted with Bourke Cochran, his mentor, who was an Irish American politician known for his oratory skills. Churchill asked Cochran, "Bourke, what is the secret of persuasion?" Cochran said, "Believing in what you are talking about."

Therefore, as a Christian minister armed with genuine faith and anointed by God to speak His truth, it would already be easier to persuade a pre-believer to listen or believe. Conversely, an observer without any strong conviction or faith, no matter how deep a knowledge such a person possess, would find it harder to persuade another.

When thinking of persuasion versus negotiation, one can think of the frequent debates between opposing politicians on national television talk shows, and it would be evident through careful observation, that the opposing politicians would continue to talk all they want, without listening, or desiring to listen to the other parties.

Therefore, a minister attempting to persuade pre-believers must be aware if he is talking more than he is listening, at least in the initial interaction phases. For example, does the minister engage the pre-believers to actively discuss, to share views, to debate, or even counter-argue fairly? Is the minister aware of what the pre-believers are genuinely looking for? Is the minister able to put aside personal prejudices or biases to present and pitch a more customized, personalized and useful message to the pre-believers?

One caveat ministers must be aware is that their human will must not interfere with God's divine will. Wiersbe said it eloquently, that ministers are but distributors of God's truth and grace, not manufacturers (Wiersbe, 15). The Holy Spirit is perhaps the truest intervention we need from God, to allow God to use us for His bidding, and it would be wise to surrender our entire will to allow Him to anoint our lips when ministering to pre-believers.

This brings us to the three personal styles of influence, which a minister may fall into one of the three, when pitching the Gospel to pre-believers. The author breaks it down into three styles, namely, persuasive, cooperating (or compromising), and aggressive.

Of the three, the persuasive style of influence is likely to create a win-win relationship with the pre-believer, and offer a higher chance of conversion to Christianity. The least successful style of influence is the aggressive style, which would likely result in heated arguments and no formation of long-term spiritually guided relationships between the minister and the pre-believer.

Persuasive style of influence

The minister first need to do a self-assessment on whether he listens to what the intended pre-believer desires, or is the minister simply saying what he wants the pre-believer to hear?

The persuasive style of influence exudes calm, reason, logic, and charisma. When a minister persuades a pre-believer in this manner, he is likely to have a win-win relationship with the pre-believer, from his intention to the end-result. When a minister persuades well, he would always look for opportunities to persuade, and legitimately take advantage of them. A minister would understand that opportunities are by nature neither good nor bad, and should be to mutual gain for the minister on behalf of God, and for the pre-believer to be brought closer to God.

The analogy of the persuasive style of influence is whereby the sum of what the minister wants to achieve and what the pre-believer wants to achieve is greater than the parts themselves. This is about a long-term relationship, and it implies that the minister should not simply persuade the pre-believer to become a convert, and thereafter no longer cares to communicate further.

The downside of a persuasive style of influence is when one is not having the best intentions and seizes control with devious means, and then it makes such a person simply manipulative and would have repercussions, for both the manipulative party, and the recipient.

Cooperative or compromising style of influence

The cooperative or compromising style of influence exudes meek compliance, and the minister is likely to end up the loser in a lose-win relationship, where the pre-believer "wins" by maintaining his stance and walks away unconvinced of the perspectives of Christianity the minister was painstakingly attempting to relay.

The analogy of such a style of influence is whereby what the minister wishes to impart to the pre-believer, and what the pre-believer wants, is equal or less than what the pre-believer truly wants or needs. This may be a situation whereby the pre-believer ends up manipulating the pitch situation, and the minister steps back from the persuasion process, and concedes on many key theological systems and orthodoxy, in order to keep the pre-believer still interested in the conversation.

In this scenario, Christian truth and teachings are sacrificed for the simple reason of maintaining continued conversation. Therefore, the end-result is the pre-believer does not benefit from orthodox Christian teachings, and walks away without much genuine knowledge, and the evangelistic process breaks down, perhaps even leaving a permanent damage to prevent the pre-believer from wishing to talk to any Christian minister in the future.

Aggressive style of influence

The aggressive style of influence is perhaps the worst of the three styles of influence. Such a style exudes anger, frustration, suspicion, and fear. The likely result is a lose-lose relationship where both the minister and the pre-believer receive nothing out of the evangelistic process. This typically happens when a minister is too aggressive to the point of irking the pre-believer to a heated argument, and both parties walk away in anger and frustration. To the pre-believer, he would be exceptionally irked because a Christian minister has been assumed to be righteous and compassionate, and should not give rise to anger.

Therefore, the pre-believer will likely be lost to the Christian evangelistic process for a long time, and will have a bitter aftertaste of Christianity due in part to the minister's personal failing in exercising restraint, as well as his failing of having compassion and an open heart when evangelizing to others.

Suggested mechanics of persuasion

The right use of subtext[98] can be useful as a tool, to assist a minister in evangelizing to pre-believers. Subtext is an outward expression of a person and may imply his personality towards another person. If the subtext of a minister can be acceptable to a pre-believer, it would be easier to persuade the pre-believer. Conversely if the subtext of a minister repulses the pre-believer, the evangelistic process will fail very quickly. The sad fact is human beings tend to be judgmental and so by understanding the context and impressions subtext can make on others, it may help ministers avoid obvious mistakes when meeting pre-believers.

The minister should as much as possible face the pre-believer squarely and maintain eye contact, which people tend to associate as an open and honest stance. Besides that, the minister can adopt a more open posture where palms are often facing the pre-believer, without such gestures as the folding of arms, or clenching of fists, which are seen as defensive or angry. Whenever possible, especially when the minister needs to make an assertive point of view, or when the pre-believer has an important view to express, lean forward. Leaning forward and closer to someone typically implies interest. The minister must also learn to relax at all times, especially during an evangelistic process. Again, a relaxed person is perceived to be honest and straightforward.

The tone of voice means different things even with the same sentence. The speed (pace) is important too, when evangelizing to people. If the minister's pace of speaking is

---

[98] Subtext can be said to be content that is communicated beneath the verbal dialog. In daily communication, subtext can mean gestures and body language.

too slow (less than 60 words per minute), the pre-believer may find the session boring, or may perceive the minister as tired or incompetent. If the minister's pace of speaking is too fast (more than 200 words per minute), the pre-believer may imagine the minister to be impatient, aggressive or rude. The pace of speaking should not be fixed too, but has fluctuation in speed according to the message at that moment. A passionate appeal or an enlightening parable may have a faster pace while difficult theological concepts that demand contemplation may require a slower pace. For example, Dr. Martin Luther King Jr.[99] spoke at a more leisurely 92 words per minute in his famous "I have a dream" speech, and ended the speech around 145 words per minute.

At the important juncture of a sentence, pauses can also be used for great effect. One would usually associate U.S. President John F Kennedy[100] and his famous "ask not what your country can do for you...(pause)... Ask what you can do for your country" speech. If he did not pause between the phrases, the result would have been very weak. Mark Twain[101] said the same thing; "There is nothing so powerful as the rightly timed pause." The pitch of speaking is important too. The lower the pitch, the more authoritative it seems to imply. A minister can sieve through national television and observe international politicians and even religious leaders making speeches, and possibly find that many of the speakers on national television tend to resonate with a lower pitch in their speeches. It is a matter

---

[99] Dr. Martin Luther King Jr. (1929 - 1968 AD) was a famous American civil rights activist and Baptist minister (Wikipedia, 2007).
[100] John Fitzgerald Kennedy (1917 - 1963 AD) was the thirty-fifth President of the United States, who was assassinated in 1963 (Wikipedia, 2007).
[101] Mark Twain was the pen name of Samuel Langhorne Clemens (1835 - 1910 AD), one of America's famous satirists, humorists and authors (Wikipedia, 2007).

of practice. Another thing that would matter is the volume of speaking. Some people speak too loudly, which can be jarring and irritating to the listener, and distract the listener from being attentive. On the other hand, if the minister speaks too softly, it would dissuade the listener to listen too. In the modern pulpit, audio-visual systems have become sophisticated and volume control is certainly possible. But in situations whereby the minister is attempting to speak to a pre-believer in social or public locations such as a street-side cafe, a garden with some human traffic, should the minister speak too softly then it would be nearly impossible for the pre-believer to be able to hear anything legible.

Having taken due consideration for non-verbal cues, a minister may also consider his choice of verbal cues and how best to position his choice and use of words, when ministering to pre-believers.

As a Christian, it is without any doubt that God has shown infinite grace and compassion throughout his journey. Therefore, for a Christian minister, it would be easy to summon an affirmative stance when attempting to persuade pre-believers. Therefore, an affirmative stance would normally mean the use of the word "when" over the word "if", since a Christian would know that God would ensure something prayed for would certainly happen, in God's time. God's providence will empower a Christian's life and so there is every reason to trust and surrender to God's will. Therefore, the word "if" would seem to yield little meaning, since God would make His providence happen for Christians.

Taking the affirmative stance a little further would be an assertive stance, in the choice of words. For example, when presenting a theological position to a pre-believer, the minister would likely choose phrases such as "I believe", rather than fumble along with words and phrases such as, "well, in my opinion..." or "I could be wrong". The minister should prepare prior to meeting the pre-believer, so that the minister should not fumble along with buffer words or redundant fillers, which may also imply a lack of confidence or conviction in the message.

Since a minister's primary objective is to create a win/win relationship with the pre-believer, it would be wise for him to always exalt the positive, rather than sink into the negative. Try to reinforce the relationship, to build on the relationship, by choosing and using the right words that do that, rather than negating the words of the pre-believers.

Although a minister may be tempted to, he may want to shy away from intensifier words such as "very", "surely", "definitely", and so on. Intensifiers tend to discredit the persuasion process and the message, since humans have mental filters to shut out and discredit such words instinctively. At the same time, if the pre-believer already has a strong opposing position, the use of such intensifier words may strengthen their opposition to the minister's message, rendering the process ineffective, or worse, agitating.

Having briefly discussed verbal expressions that may hamper a minister's communication with pre-believers, there are ways to win pre-believers over with persuasive language.

For example, Cao Cao[102], one of the great military strategists in ancient China, was escaping the onslaught of a larger enemy, and most of his solders were dehydrated. Cao Cao then told his soldiers that just a short distance ahead, was a large plantation of prunes. Cao Cao's soldiers immediately became more energized, because the thought of sour prunes was enough to cause salivation, and they

---

[102] Cao Cao (155 – 220 AD) was a warlord and chancellor of the Eastern Han Dynasty during the Three Kingdoms period (Wikipedia, 2007).

soldiered on. Was there actually a prune plantation? No. But by instilling hope in his soldiers he managed to save them from death.

Likewise, when a minister intends to persuade, he may use vivid language, rather than simply quoting statistics and stoic data. Some of the effective secular communicators such as U.S. President John F Kennedy, President Ronald Reagan[103], President Bill Clinton[104], former British Premier Tony Blair[105], and Dr. Martin Luther King Jr., are familiar names who used language that stirred and fired up the imagination of their intended audiences, rather than simply relying on cold, hard facts. Metaphors are a more advanced verbal tool that demands skill and practice. For example, people used to describe former British Premier Margaret Thatcher[106] as the "Iron Lady", and immediately people's minds conjure up the image of a "tough-as-nails" politician who meant business. A relative of metaphors is analogy. For example, one can say, "An analogy of the crowded room of people is like a bowl full of hot corn in the process of popping." If a minister can deliver metaphors and analogies

---

[103] Ronald Wilson Reagan (1911 – 2004 AD) was the 40th President of the United States, one of the noted orators in America. He was also an accomplished actor before he took the presidential office (Wikipedia, 2007).

[104] William Jefferson "Bill" Clinton (born 1946 AD) was the 42nd President of the United States, also a noted orator. He was a law professor and then governor of Arkansas before he took the presidential office (Wikipedia, 2007).

[105] Anthony Charles Lynton Blair (born 1953 AD) served as the Prime Minister of the United Kingdom from 1997 to 2007, and was the leader of the British Labor Party till 2007. He is now an Envoy of the United Nations (UN) and European Union (EU) to the Middle East (Wikipedia, 2007).

[106] Margaret Hilda Thatcher, Baroness Thatcher (born 1925 AD) served as the Prime Minister of the United Kingdom from 1979 to 1990, and was the leader of the British Conservative Party till 1990 (Wikipedia, 2007).

well, he is almost certainly a storyteller, much as our beloved Lord Jesus Christ did. Stories can create atmosphere, mood, and stimulation, enough to get an audience captivated in listening intently.

The process of attempting to persuade pre-believers must never be made personal. Although a minister must stake his claim always, on theological orthodoxy and faith, he should not attempt to simply rely on emotive passion to win pre-believers over. Often, even if a momentary passion is able to win converts, such conversion may be short-lived. At other times, the passionate call to conversion may irk pre-believers, especially in locations such as Asia where rich, long and diverse traditions and beliefs predate many of modern Christianity's paths, and objections would often be raised. The minister must learn as much as possible about his pre-believers, much as Jesuit priest Matteo Ricci did with the Chinese, in order to win friends and allies, and thereafter, converts, and then, disciples of Christ.

Conclusions

Evangelizing God's Word to pre-believers is getting more complex and difficult these days, especially in a richly diverse and increasingly unforgiving world we live in today.

While we earnestly seek to do God's work in various locations around the world, it dawns on us, as God's humble servants, that it will demand the best and the noblest out of ministers, to be able to render as humane, compassionate, and loving a form of evangelism as possible to pre-believers, especially in Asia. Philip Brooks was quoted, "Do not pray for easy lives; pray to be stronger men! Do not pray for tasks equal to your powers. Pray for powers equal to your tasks. Then the doing of your work shall be no miracle, but you shall be a miracle" (Osbeck, 293).

We have observed from a rich lineage and history of Christian evangelism throughout the ages, including Asia, which benefited from many of the finest Christian missionaries who poured their hearts and souls to help others embrace Christianity, sometimes sacrificing their well-being and even lives, to further God's Will. While such admirable predecessors abound in our history, the author has chosen the Jesuit priest Matteo Ricci, as well as contemporary Trappist monk Thomas Merton, as some examples of how such fine Christians have managed to bridge Asian thought and cultures, with orthodox Christian thought, and remained steadfast and committed to God and God's Word.

The author, through extensive study of various Asian philosophies, have uncovered possibilities of explaining some of the fundamental thought with a Christian focus and theme, including the concepts of "karma", or cause and effect. While some may focus on divergence and complex differences, the author has seen how some of our predecessors such as Matteo Ricci have managed to find similarities and Gospel-centric methods of explaining the differences to allow pre-believers in Asia to make sense of Christianity, and ultimately accepting Christ.

At the same time, the author asserted that there would be a need to minister to different communities differently, using the three strategic and tactical paths of Works, Evangelism, and Brotherhood. By helping the disenfranchised and disadvantaged in the communities through humanitarian works, Christian ministers can show themselves as the light of the world. With those who are seeking spiritual awareness, evangelism would be the best vehicle to help bring those pre-believers into the cradle of Christianity. And for pre-believers who may be highly successful and somewhat more skeptical or critical, the use of fraternity and brotherhood may be a method to engage their interest, through collaborative community service.

The author illustrated the evangelism as a process, which he defined as "Historical, Obstacle, Projection, and End-results (or H.O.P.E.)". Through fact-finding and investigation of the History and needs of a pre-believer, the minister is able to arm himself with prerequisite knowledge to demonstrate to the pre-believer of his interest in helping the pre-believer. Next, when facing the pre-believer, the minister needs to overcome Obstacles including theological debate. Next, when the minister is able to get through the obstacles, he can witness for Christ through the Projection step, by showing the pre-believer the fruition of faith and discipleship in Christ. At the end, the minister would achieve the End-results of converting the pre-believer to embrace Christianity.

In Asia, where assertiveness is often not the best way to persuade people, the author explained that using the persuasive style of influence is much more effective at winning converts then simply compromising the Christian position, or worse, using aggression as the hopeful means to batter the pre-believer to submission. Christian theology and the Bible are not simply parables and stories to read and forget, but contain infinite wisdom of God that can transform lives permanently. Sometimes, perhaps "baby steps" may be sufficient to help pre-believers begin to think through and get curious about Christianity. At the end of the day, all that matters is a simple message to pre-believers, that Jesus Christ our Lord came, and sacrificed Himself for our redemption. That in itself, a universal love and compassion message, is the ultimate story to tell, in as few words and as simple as possible a way, and would appeal to everyone. Archibald Alexander said it so succinctly, "All my theology is reduced to this narrow compass - Christ Jesus came into this world to save sinners" (Osbeck, 90).

As his Lutheran bishop reminded the author that the path of being a minister is a long, painful and arduous process, a minister must be prepared to fail, in many of the situations when attempting to evangelize to pre-believers. God in His infinite wisdom is often the final arbiter on when and how believers will join His kingdom, and the role of the minister is that of God's facilitator and diplomat.

The author humbly believes as a Christian that if science and logic fail to explain the statistically unlikely or the impossible, then whatever remains must be of God. The author has faced personal struggles and challenges that presented many personal miracles from God that led the author to be convinced of the irresistible grace of God. The author hopes, with the same infinite grace of God, that as a bi-vocational minister he will be able to continue to lead and partake in the administration of humanitarian works for the underprivileged communities, to evangelize to the seekers of truth, and brotherhood with the accomplished to form a trusted platform for more expanded works for others for the sake of glorifying God.

In closing, the author frequently refers to the prayer of Saint Francis of Assisi, titled "Instrument of Peace". The author's humble opinion is that Saint Francis' prayer summarizes the spectrum of emotions and actions that would work in practical terms, when ministering and evangelizing to the pre-believers in difficult locations, such as in Asia. Saint Francis' words showed that in the midst of hatred, Christians could show love in return, as love pacifies hate. In the midst of discord among communities, Christians can attempt to unite. In many underprivileged or disenfranchised locations in Asia where food, simple lodging, and clean water are absent, Christians can bring hope, joy and light to them. At the utmost ideal of a Christian minister, as emissary and diplomat for Christ, he can be God's instrument for peace.

Lord, make me an instrument of Thy peace.
Where there is hatred, let me sow love.
Where there is injury, pardon.
Where there is discord, unity.
Where there is doubt, faith.
Where there is error, truth.
Where there is despair, hope.
Where there is sadness, joy.
Where there is darkness, light.
For it is in giving, that we receive.
It is in pardoning, that we are pardoned.
It is in dying, that we are born to eternal life.

Bibliography

Darby, John Nelson. Darby Bible version 1.1. A literal translation of the Old Testament (1890) and the New Testament (1884). Public Domain, 1889.

Challoner, Richard. Douay-Rheims Bible, Challoner Revision. Translated from the Latin Vulgate, diligently compared with the Hebrew, Greek and other editions in Divers languages. Public Domain, 1749-1752.

Rhodes, Ron. The Complete Guide to Christian Denominations – Understanding the History, Beliefs, and Differences. Oregon: Harvest House Publishers, 2005.

Second Vatican Council, Wikipedia, accessed from http://en.wikipedia.org/wiki/Second_Vatican_Council, on June 18, 2007.

The 95 Theses by Martin Luther, Center for Reformed Theology and Apologetics (CRTA), access from http://www.reformed.org/documents/95_theses.html, on June 18, 2007.

Abuses of indulgences, Wikipedia, accessed from http://en.wikipedia.org/wiki/Abuses_of_Indulgences, on June 18, 2007.

The Book of Concord, Internet, accessed from http://www.bookofconcord.org, on June 18, 2007.

Peterson, Eugene H. The Contemplative Pastor – Returning to the Art of Spiritual Direction. Michigan: Wm. B. Eerdmans Publishing Co, 1993.

Wilken, Robert Louis. The Spirit of Early Christian Thought: Seeking the Face of God. Virginia: Yale University Press, 2003.

Saint Augustine – Stanford Encyclopedia of Philosophy, accessed from http://plato.stanford.edu/entries/augustine/, on July 10, 2007.

Lewis, Clive Staples. Mere Christianity. New York: HarperCollins Publishers Inc., 2001.

Big Bang, access from http://en.wikipedia.org/wiki/Big_Bang, on July 25, 2007.

Erickson, Millard J. Christian Theology. Michigan: Baker Academic, 2006.

Rieff, Philip. Charisma: The Gift of Grace, and how it has been taken away from us. New York: Pantheon Books, 2007.

Webber, Robert E.. The Complete Library of Christian Worship, Vol. 6, The Sacred Actions of Christian Worship. Massachusetts: Hendrickson Publishers, Inc., 1993.

McGrath, Alister E. The Christian theology reader. Massachusetts: Blackwell Publishing, 2007.

Erickson, Millard J. Christian Theology. Michigan: Baker Academic, 2006.

Dillard, John R. On the Eucharist in the context of Celtic Christianity. Email, November 27, 2007.

Tertullian, accessed from http://en.wikipedia.org/wiki/Tertullian, on November 30, 2007.

Didache early Christian treatise on rituals such as baptism and the Eucharist, accessed from http://en.wikipedia.org/wiki/Didache, on November 30, 2007.

The 95 Theses by Martin Luther, Center for Reformed Theology and Apologetics (CRTA), access from http://www.reformed.org/documents/95_theses.html, on June 18, 2007.

Rives, James B. Religion in the Roman Empire. Massachusetts: Blackwell Publishing, 2007.

Armstrong, Karen. The Bible: A Biography. New York: Grove Atlantic Ltd., 2007.

Dillard, John R. On the impact of Constantine on the evolution of Christianity. Email, December 3, 2007.

Dillard, John R. On Johannine Celtic Christianity and Characteristics. Paper, November 11, 2007.

Dillard, John R. On the Holy Celtic Apostolic Church and its History. Paper, November 11, 2007.

Dillard, John R. On the Early Church. Paper, November 11, 2007.

St. John of Ephesus, accessed from http://en.wikipedia.org/wiki/John_of_Ephesus, on December 4, 2007.

Christmas and its various influences, accessed from http://en.wikipedia.org/wiki/Christmas, on December 4, 2007.

Sol Invictus and its various influences on Christmas, accessed from http://en.wikipedia.org/wiki/Sol_Invictus, on December 4, 2007.

Puritans and their beliefs of seeking purity in worship, accessed from http://en.wikipedia.org/wiki/Puritan, on December 4, 2007.

Separation of Church and State, accessed from http://en.wikipedia.org/wiki/Separation_of_Church_and_State, on December 4, 2007.

Constantinianism, accessed from http://en.wikipedia.org/wiki/Constantinianism, on December 4, 2007.

Arianism, accessed from http://en.wikipedia.org/wiki/Arianism, on December 4, 2007.

Caesaropapism, accessed from http://en.wikipedia.org/wiki/Caesaropapism, on December 4, 2007.

Constantine I and Christianity, accessed from http://en.wikipedia.org/wiki/Constantine_I_and_Christianity, on December 4, 2007.

Constantinian Shift, accessed from http://en.wikipedia.org/wiki/Constantinian_shift, on December 4, 2007.

Easter and its controversy, accessed from http://en.wikipedia.org/wiki/Easter, on December 4, 2007.

Synod and Council of Arles and the Donatist heresy in 314 AD, accessed from http://en.wikipedia.org/wiki/Synod_of_Arles, on December 4, 2007.

Willard, Dallas. The Great Omission: Reclaiming Jesus's Essential Teachings on Discipleship. HarperCollins e-books, 2006.

Spiritual Direction and concepts, Spiritual Directional International (SDI World), accessed from http://www.sdiworld.org/what_is_spiritual_direction2.html, on June 28, 2007. Wright, Jonathan. The Jesuits: Missions, Myths and Histories. London: Harper Perennial, 2004.

Aikman, David. Jesus in Beijing: How Christianity is Transforming China and Changing the Global Balance of Power. Oxford: Monarch Books, 2003.

Gelber, Harry G. The Dragon and the Foreign Devils: China and the World, 1100 BC to the Present. London: Bloomsbury Publishing Plc, 2007.

Prime, Derek, and Begg, Alistair. On Being a Pastor: Understanding Our Calling and Work. Chicago: Moody Publishers, 2004.

Trigilio Jr., John, Brighenti, Kenneth, and Wiggins, James B. 101 Things Everyone Should Know about the Bible. Massachusetts: Adams Media, 2006.

Osbeck, Kenneth W. Amazing Grace: 366 Inspiring Hymn Stories for Daily Devotions. Michigan: Kregel Publications, 2002.

Wiersbe, Warren W. On being a servant of God. Michigan: Baker Books, 1993.

McGlone, Lee. The Minister's Manual 2008. San Francisco: Jossey-Bass, 2007.

Willard, Dallas. The Divine Conspiracy: Rediscovering Our Hidden Life in God. New York: HarperCollins Publishers, 1997.

Pagels, Elaine. The Origin of Satan. New York: Vintage Books, 1995.

Owen, Harrison. Open space technology: a user's guide. San Francisco: Berrett-Koehler Publishers, Inc., 1997.

Erickson, Millard J. Christian Theology. Michigan: Baker Academic, 2006.

Collins, Francis. The Language of God: A Scientist Presents Evidence for Belief. London: Pocket Books, 2007.

Matteo Ricci, Wikipedia, accessed from http://en.wikipedia.org/wiki/Matteo_Ricci, and http://zh.wikipedia.org/wiki/利玛窦 (translated as "li ma dou") on August 16, 2007.

Matteo Ricci, Catholic Encyclopedia, accessed from http://www.newadvent.org/cathen/13034a.htm, on August 16, 2007.

Jesuits, The Society of Jesus in the United States, accessed from http://www.jesuit.org/, on August 16, 2007.

Society of Jesus, Wikipedia, accessed from http://en.wikipedia.org/wiki/Society_of_Jesus, on August 16, 2007.

The Jesuits (Society of Jesus), Catholic Encyclopedia, accessed from http://www.newadvent.org/cathen/14081a.htm, on August 16, 2007.

Jesuit Mathematicians and Jesuit Scientists, Fairfield University, accessed from http://www.faculty.fairfield.edu/jmac/sj/sjscient.htm, on August 16, 2007.

A Pictorial History of the Jesuits, Fairfield University, accessed from http://www.faculty.fairfield.edu/jmac/sj/sjhist.htm, on August 16, 2007.

Jesuit China Missions, Wikipedia, accessed from http://en.wikipedia.org/wiki/Jesuit_China_missions, on August 16, 2007.

Thomas Merton, Wikipedia, accessed from http://en.wikipedia.org/wiki/Thomas_Merton, August 30, 2007.

Thomas Merton, O.C.S.O., accessed from http://www.geocities.com/ganesha_gate/merton.html, on August 30, 2007.

William Chalmers Burns, Wikipedia, accessed from http://en.wikipedia.org/wiki/William_Chalmers_Burns, on September 2, 2007.

Servants to Asia's Urban Poor, Wikipedia, accessed from http://en.wikipedia.org/wiki/Servants_to_Asia%27s_Urban_Poor, on August 30, 2007.

Milarepa, his life, Kagyud Asia, accessed from http://www.kagyu-asia.com/l_mila_life1.html, on September 24, 2007.

Jetsun Milarepa, Tibet's most famous meditator, ROKPA, accessed from http://www.samye.org/mila.htm, on September 24, 2007.

Fang xia tu dao, li di chen fuo (leave the butcher's knife behind and become enlightened), Earth Store Net, accessed from http://www.dizang.org/wd/hh/018.htm, accessed from August 30, 2007.

Open Space Technology (OST), Wikipedia, accessed from http://en.wikipedia.org/wiki/Open_Space_Technology, on September 24, 2007.

Nestorian.org, accessed from http://www.nestorian.org/unofficial_home_page_of_the_on.html, on September 24, 2007.

Papers "Theology of the forms of Christian life in the chuch", by Fr. Domingo Moraleda Molero CMF, Institute for Consecrated Life in Asia (ICLA), Pontifical University of Santo Tomas.

Phan, Seamus. Major Account Generation and Investigative Program. Training Program, 2001.

Phan, Seamus. Persuade your way to the top! Training Program, 2001.

Index

14-Nisan.................................. 133
95 Theses............ 14, 175, 223, 224
Abraham..................................... 40
Adventist 8, 10, 121
Alopen 174
Ambrose 51, 125
Anabaptists 11
Anglican..... 8, 9, 10, 13, 15, 40, 99, 119, 121, 123, 201
apocalyptic 23, 27, 35
apologetic.................... 8, 40, 55, 84
apologist..... 39, 40, 59, 61, 86, 119
Apostle's Creed 81, 87
Apostles' Creed 14, 43, 45, 56, 175
Archbishop of Canterbury......... 13
Arminian 11, 16, 17, 18, 87, 96
Augsburg Confession 15, 175
Baptist.............. 8, 11, 94, 121, 213
Beatitudes 22, 54, 182, 188
Boniface 50
Calvinist............... 10, 11, 18, 29, 87
Catechism..................... 14, 18, 175
Catholic 8, 9, 11, 12, 14, 16, 18, 38, 39, 40, 41, 42, 43, 45, 46, 47, 50, 54, 81, 93, 99, 100, 111, 118, 119, 120, 121, 122, 123, 124, 125, 128, 132, 133, 134, 171, 174, 175, 183, 227
charisma.. 106, 107, 108, 109, 111, 112, 113, 114, 115, 192, 209
Clement of Alexandria...... 42, 118, 124, 125
communion 13, 14, 27, 29, 30, 31, 36, 43, 64, 80, 87, 89, 92, 93, 132, 137, 163, 202, 203
Confucian Analects.................. 184
CS Lewis 57, 58
Dalai Lama 183, 184
De Trinitate 46
Denominations 7, 8, 21, 37, 57, 77, 105, 117, 127, 139, 157, 167, 223
dichotomism.............................. 90
Didache 120, 121, 124, 224
Donatist.................... 131, 132, 226
dualism 62
Easter............... 132, 134, 135, 226
Ephesians........... 33, 119, 191, 192
Episcopal...................... 8, 9, 13, 99
Eucharist . 12, 41, 45, 52, 118, 119, 120, 122, 123, 124, 224
Eugene Peterson 22
Evagrius................................ 40, 56
evangelism... 39, 78, 135, 165, 168, 171, 180, 183, 184, 190, 194, 195, 196, 197, 217, 218, 219
ex cathedra 16
Freud 66, 106, 109, 112
Galatians ... 54, 110, 160, 169, 170, 187
Genesis....... 48, 84, 86, 87, 88, 124, 204
glossolalia 17, 95, 96
Gnosticism................................. 42
Harrison Owen........................ 198
Holy Spirit .. 11, 15, 17, 31, 43, 44, 45, 46, 52, 54, 55, 56, 71, 78, 86, 87, 95, 97, 101, 102, 120, 121, 122, 131, 160, 203, 205, 206, 209
Ignatius Loyola 54, 174
Irenaeus..... 43, 118, 123, 124, 125, 133
Jesuits 54, 136, 174, 175, 178, 179, 180, 181, 226, 227
Jesus Christ ... 8, 10, 11, 12, 14, 15, 38, 39, 42, 43, 45, 46, 47, 49, 53, 71, 72, 86, 90, 93, 94, 95, 100, 101, 102, 109, 118, 121, 125, 128, 129, 131, 132, 134, 168, 170, 171, 173, 189, 199, 201, 217, 219
Johannine 120, 121, 128, 129, 130, 132, 133, 135, 224
John Calvin. 10, 17, 29, 78, 83, 85, 90
John Nelson Darby.. 10, 14, 33, 99
Judaism 8, 12, 39, 44, 62, 86
Justin Martyr 39, 118
karma 136, 186, 187, 218
Lutheran . 8, 9, 14, 18, 72, 81, 100, 121, 123, 164, 175, 220

Maccabees 43
Marpa 189
marriage 13, 41, 67, 119, 124
Martin Luther 9, 14, 18, 38, 78, 80, 83, 90, 100, 111, 123, 124, 162, 175, 213, 216, 223, 224
Martin Luther King Jr. 213
Matteo Ricci ... 136, 168, 169, 172, 174, 176, 182, 184, 192, 217, 218, 227
Methodist 8, 10, 15, 121, 122
Michael Caerularius 9
Michele Ruggieri 176
Milarepa 188, 189, 228
Modernism 82
Narnia 59
Nestorius 47, 173
New Testament . 12, 17, 33, 42, 66, 81, 120, 158, 168, 223
Nicaea 44, 47, 131, 133
Nicene Creed .. 14, 15, 44, 56, 175
Old Catholic 11, 13
Old Testament 8, 12, 33, 42, 52, 86, 95, 97, 98, 123, 133, 223
Open Space Technology .. 198, 228
Origen 39, 40, 43, 44, 135
Orthodox .. 8, 9, 11, 12, 13, 16, 18, 38, 40, 41, 43, 45, 83, 84, 86, 93, 99, 107, 118, 121, 123, 124, 128, 134, 173, 174
Pantheism 62, 74
Paul Tillich 86
Pauline 128, 129, 132, 133, 135
Pentecostal 8, 10, 17, 19, 121
Pope Clement VII 13
Pope Clement VIII 42
Pope John Paul II 83
Pope Leo I 9, 12
Pope Martin 48

Presbyterian .. 8, 10, 17, 22, 23, 24, 34, 99, 121
Protestant .. 8, 9, 10, 11, 12, 14, 16, 18, 38, 41, 45, 78, 86, 93, 109, 118, 119, 120, 121, 122, 124, 125, 133, 136, 175
Protestantism .. 9, 10, 54, 107, 111, 174, 175
Resurrection 45, 47, 132
Robert Louis Wilken 38
Rotary 193, 194
Rudolf Bultmann 81
Runge 189
sacraments 12, 38, 64, 110, 118, 119, 120, 124, 125, 132
Saint Augustine 40, 41, 46, 49, 56, 58, 223
Saint Francis of Assissi 162
Saint Francis Xavier 175
Saint Teresa of Avila 164
Satan 62, 63, 69, 227
sinner 32, 69, 92, 193
Society of Jesus ... 54, 174, 175, 227
spiritual direction ... 22, 24, 25, 27, 28, 30, 31, 32, 34, 35, 36, 54
Spiritual Directors International 24
Syncretism 180, 181
Tertullian 118, 119, 224
Thomas Merton 183, 218, 228
transubstantiation 100, 123
Trappist 183, 218
Triune God . 14, 15, 38, 41, 44, 46, 71, 102, 114, 131
Utrecht 13
Wesley 10, 15, 159, 162, 164
William Chalmers Burns . 192, 228
Winston Churchill 208
Word of God 49, 50, 53, 56, 98, 99, 111, 129, 131, 160, 170, 181, 190, 206

About the Author

Fr. Seamus Phan is a bi-vocational ordained Christian orthodox priest and writer. Fr. Seamus graduated with a theology degree through distance learning at Newburgh Theological Seminary. Fr. Seamus focuses on spiritual direction and the written word ministry.

Fr. Seamus' secular role is a professional speaker, corporate educator, adjunct professor of economics and sustainable development, journalist, and writer. He has been a corporate educator and communicator since the 1980s. He earned a doctor of business administration, specializing in the use of Internet server technologies and business process analysis.

www.ingramcontent.com/pod-product-compliance
Lightning Source LLC
Chambersburg PA
CBHW051751040426
42446CB00007B/318